"*Choosing Brilliant Health* shows us how to make very reality-based choices about personal health. This book is so basic, and with so much common sense, that it should be part of every elementary school curriculum. Not only is it grounded in the science gleaned from recent studies about mind-body medicine, but also in the real-life stories of diverse people from all over the world. *Choosing Brilliant Health* works!"

—David Roche, author of *The Church of 80% Sincerity*

"The brilliant choice is to read this book! *Choosing Brilliant Health* powerfully reveals that health is a verb, not just an office visit or medical treatment. The book is a wonderfully constructed guide for something already within each of us: intentionally chosen and actively lived mind, body, and spirit."

—Jody Hereford, former President of the American Association of Cardiovascular and Pulmonary Rehabilitation

"*Choosing Brilliant Health* reinforces why personal accountability is such an important key to success in every aspect of our lives. With their inspiring and practical book, Foster and Hicks make a vital contribution to the understanding of using positive thoughts, emotions, and behaviors to promote well-being."

—John G. Miller, author of *QBQ! The Question Behind the Question* and *Flipping the Switch*

continued . . .

Choosing Brilliant Health

9 Choices That Redefine What It Takes to
Create Lifelong Vitality and Well-Being

RICK FOSTER AND GREG HICKS

WITH JEN SEDA, MD

A Perigee Book

A PERIGEE BOOK
Published by the Penguin Group
Penguin Group (USA) Inc.
375 Hudson Street, New York, New York 10014, USA
Penguin Group (Canada), 90 Eglinton Avenue East, Suite 700, Toronto, Ontario M4P 2Y3, Canada (a division of Pearson Penguin Canada Inc.) • Penguin Books Ltd., 80 Strand, London WC2R 0RL, England • Penguin Group Ireland, 25 St. Stephen's Green, Dublin 2, Ireland (a division of Penguin Books Ltd.) • Penguin Group (Australia), 250 Camberwell Road, Camberwell, Victoria 3124, Australia (a division of Pearson Australia Group Pty. Ltd.) • Penguin Books India Pvt. Ltd., 11 Community Centre, Panchsheel Park, New Delhi—110 017, India • Penguin Group (NZ), 67 Apollo Drive, Rosedale, North Shore 0632, New Zealand (a division of Pearson New Zealand Ltd.) • Penguin Books (South Africa) (Pty.) Ltd., 24 Sturdee Avenue, Rosebank, Johannesburg 2196, South Africa

Penguin Books Ltd., Registered Offices: 80 Strand, London WC2R 0RL, England

While the authors have made every effort to provide accurate telephone numbers and Internet addresses at the time of publication, neither the publisher nor the authors assume any responsibility for errors, or for changes that occur after publication. Further, the publisher does not have any control over and does not assume any responsibility for author or third-party websites or their content.

First edition: May 2008

Library of Congress Cataloging-in-Publication Data

Foster, Rick, 1949–
  Choosing brilliant health : 9 choices that redefine what it takes to create lifelong vitality and well-being / Rick Foster & Greg Hicks with Jen Seda.
     p. cm.
  Includes bibliographical references and index.
  ISBN 978-0-399-53420-1
  1. Health. 2. Health—Psychological aspects. 3. Happiness. 4. Mind and body. 5. Self-care, Health. I. Hicks, Greg, 1953– II. Seda, Jen. III. Title.
  RA776.5.F673 2008
   613—dc22   2007048303

PRINTED IN THE UNITED STATES OF AMERICA

10 9 8 7 6 5 4 3 2 1

PUBLISHER'S NOTE: Neither the publisher nor the authors are engaged in rendering professional advice or services to the individual reader. The ideas, procedures, and suggestions contained in this book are not intended as a substitute for consulting with your physician. All matters regarding your health require medical supervision. Neither the authors nor the publisher shall be liable or responsible for any loss or damage allegedly arising from any information or suggestion in this book.

Most Perigee books are available at special quantity discounts for bulk purchases for sales promotions, premiums, fund-raising, or educational use. Special books, or book excerpts, can also be created to fit specific needs. For details, write: Special Markets, Penguin Group (USA) Inc., 375 Hudson Street, New York, New York 10014.

To our parents:

Diana and Harold Foster,
whose skill at growing older with grace
is surpassed only by their generosity of spirit.

Lenore and Don Hicks,
loving and involved parents and grandparents,
whose value of family has enhanced the lives of many.

ACKNOWLEDGMENTS

We're fortunate to have a big, wonderful, exuberant, and very intentional community of colleagues and friends who contributed to the Brilliant Health journey in their own unique ways.

From the medical and research world, we'd like to thank:

The Mayo Clinic, which gave our work and research such extraordinary support, especially the Department of Nursing whose leadership team has more letters after their names than can be listed here: Doreen Frusti, Jackie Attlesey-Pries, Sharon Tucker, Diane Twedell, and the entire NEC team; and the Department of Medicine: Drs. Brent Bauer, David Rosenman, Randal Thomas, Jeanne Huddleston; and Kristin Vickers-Douglas, PhD; Jeff Sloan, PhD; and Natasha Matt-Hensrud.

New York University Medical Center, especially Bernard Birnbaum, MD, Vice Dean and Chief of Hospital Operations, who was both generous and influential in our thinking about the kind of medical perspective we needed; Elizabeth Duthie, PhD, Director of Patient Safety, who is an innovator, a bottomless well of information, and a "medical angel" to us and our families; and the team at the Office of Development and Learning, who have been fun and wonderful partners, in particular Richard Woodrow, Lori Burkhoff, and Martin Costa.

Duffy Newman, Director of the Health Research and Educational Trust's Fellowship Programs, and her dedicated staff, who have facilitated our work as faculty with top medical professionals from around the world.

Aileen Killen, PhD, currently Director of the Patient Safety Program and formerly Director of Perioperative Nursing at Sloan-Kettering Memorial Cancer Center; and David Jaques, MD, Vice President of surgical services at Barnes-Jewish Hospital—friends and colleagues for many years, who gave us a rare entrée into the world of surgery and surgical teams.

The Actors' Fund of America, a terrific organization that gave us the opportunity to conduct our first Brilliant Health workshops for the chronically and terminally ill over the course of two years, especially Barbara Davis, Keith McNutt, Carol Mannes, Roz Gilbert, Tamar Shapiro, and Joe Benincasa.

Drs. Mmbara Nkhangweni, Harry Moultrie, and Angela Maloka, RN, all specialists in the treatment of HIV/AIDS, who hosted us at Baragwanath Hospital in Johannesburg as presenters to one of the most resilient and perceptive groups of medical specialists we've ever met and who taught us about things we had never imagined.

Roger Schimberg, a new friend, who took us under his wing in South Africa, navigated the back roads with us, and introduced us to the unforgettable array of AIDS organizations with whom we had the honor to work.

Mary Sue Moore, PhD in Clinical Psychology with a research specialty in the effects of emotional trauma on brain development, who arrived right in the heart of our writer's despair, bringing both her incredible knowledge of the brain *and* dark chocolates.

Dr. Catherine Bannerman, Medical Director of Palliative Care and Hospice at Torrance Memorial Medical Center, and members of her staff including Dana Hodgdon, MA, and Mary Carolla, RN, who shared years of perceptions about end-of-life care during a series of moving interviews.

Catherine O'Brien, PhD, Assistant Professor at the School of Education, Health, and Wellness, and Rhonda MacCormick, Director of the Health Research Centre, both at Cape Breton University in Nova Scotia, who opened up exciting research opportunities and brought us together with the Mi'kmaq Tribal Elders to exchange happiness philosophies and ideas.

Diane Tedeschi, Michael Mutter, and Linda Malkin, at the Valley Hospital in Ridgewood, New Jersey, a dynamic trio of experts on patient care, quality, and risk management, respectively, who have become great friends and advocates.

Alan H. Rosenstein, MD, Vice President and Medical Director of VHA West Coast, and Patricia Tyler, Director of Performance Improvement, VHA, who shared ideas and came through with irreplaceable introductions.

James Baraz, founding teacher of Spirit Rock Meditation Center and creator of the "Awakening Joy" class, who took our happiness model in entirely new directions, and, along with Edith Politis, introduced us to the Realm of the Hungry Ghost.

Sarah Hue-Williams and Emily Morrow, cofounders of the Patient Coach in Sydney, Australia.

Acknowledgments

Tom Miller and his staff at the National Research Center in Boulder, Colorado, who brought our research statistics to life.

From the realm of writing, we thank:

John Duff, our trusted friend and editor extraordinaire at Penguin, who nurtured our book so carefully and brilliantly through each phase and was the ultimate collaborative partner.

Jim Nawrocki, our very talented wordsmith and story-telling editor, who jumped in with total commitment at the eleventh hour, and Dick Ridington, who lent fresh editorial insights as well.

Our manuscript readers, all of whom brought their distinct background and opinions to early versions of the book: Lenore and Don Hicks; Cathy Hicks; Diana and Hal Foster; Laurie and Mark Grassman, MSW; Genesse Gentry; and Alex Feng, LAc, PhD, OMD, and Charlene Ossler, RN, PhD, from Zhi Dao Guan, the Taoist Center in Oakland, California.

We also want to offer appreciation to those who were our life-supporters throughout the twists and turns of the Brilliant Health odyssey and who each played a role in shaping this book: Ellen Tussman, Diane Jarmolow, Peter Tamases, Tim Mitchell, Janet Cobb, Paul and Helen Canin, Marilyn Ginsburg, Herb Kindler, Barrie Hathaway, Lisa Schilling, Brian Stone, Karen Rae Wilson, Bob Levine, Mark McCormick, Russell Kaltschmidt, Eva Nemeth, Tim Ware, Olive Hackett-Shaunessy, and Karen Freidman; and Jen's family, Ben Wisner, Catherine Seda, and Irene Seda.

Acknowledgments

We're especially grateful to our passionate, creative, and engaged adult children, Tim Hicks, Molly Hicks, Kat Foster, and Alex Foster. Beyond genetics, we can't really take credit for how wonderful they are—they are truly their own creations. We thank them for their love and for indulging their crazy, idea-chasing fathers, and want to tell them that they are our greatest inspiration and joy.

Finally, we are forever in debt to the many people around the world—patients, physicians, nurses, and medical specialists—who gave us their stories and insights with such honesty and compassion. And to the members of our Brilliant Health workshops, who shared their experiences and breakthroughs so willingly and graciously, and from whom we learned so much. We promised all of you anonymity and privacy. You know who you are and we want to thank you from our hearts.

—Greg Hicks and Rick Foster
Berkeley, California

AUTHORS' NOTE

We believe deeply in current attitudes about patient privacy, and we promised anonymity to the people who shared their stories so generously. To that end we have changed the names and locations of nearly all the interviewees, nurses, doctors, medical facilities, and other professionals you'll read about in the following pages.

The information in *Choosing Brilliant Health* is not intended to serve as a replacement for professional medical advice. We want to encourage our readers to use its concepts along with the best of other effective health practices.

Every patient carries her or his own doctor inside.

—ALBERT SCHWEITZER (1875–1965)

CONTENTS

Contents

PART ONE

Embracing
Brilliant Health

You're about to discover how to take control of your health in a revolutionary way. You won't need to buy anything, take anything, or eat anything different. What you'll need is already within you: the thoughts and behaviors that create positive emotions.

This book will help you experience the extraordinary physical power of positive emotions and use them to achieve Brilliant Health. Brilliant Health is a sensation. It's a deep feeling of vitality, well-being, and the sense that you've achieved the highest possible quality of life. When you live in Brilliant Health, you have a healthier body down to the cellular level. You have better brain function. You recover faster from illness and injury. Your organ systems function better. And you can even look forward to the possibility of a longer, and definitely better, life.

Of the many things we do to manage our health, training ourselves to recognize and nurture the positive emotions that create Brilliant Health is the least utilized yet most powerful of all. And anyone, regardless of age, background, genetics, or health status, can implement its nine life-changing practices.

We have spent the last thirteen years uncovering what makes people happy and, with the help of medical researchers, finding out how happiness also makes us healthier, whether we're battling illness or simply trying to achieve maximal health. Although there's been an upsurge of coverage in the popular press about connecting our emotions to our physical health, you're reading the first practical road map for achieving that connection.

We all know negative emotions like stress, anxiety, anger, and depression are bad for us. But only now is twenty-first-century medical research substantiating what our grandmothers told us, and what the ancients have known for ages: positive attitude benefits your health. Scientists currently report that happiness (many researchers call it "positive affect") not only precedes good health, but is a root cause of good health. You may not be totally surprised that scientists can now prove happiness correlates strongly with behavioral and mental health benefits, such as higher pain thresholds, better adherence to treatments, and healthier life choices like diet and exercise. But what may surprise you is science can also substantiate that happiness improves physical responses such as better heart attack survival rates, reduced incidence of stroke, enhanced natural killer-cell activity in cancer patients, less intense allergic reactions, and better resistance to colds.

Though immensely exciting in theory, translating this research into practice has, until now, been frustrating at best. Most of us believe statements like, "Her good attitude really helped with her recovery." But what does that really mean, and how do we get these positive mind-sets for ourselves? It's a bit like wanting to go to Disneyland but being stuck in Siberia without a map. Even researchers who credit positive affect as a major driver of good health admit to not knowing if it's just something you're born with, or, if not, how to get it.

Currently, science makes advances by investigating a single domain, such as a gene, a specific reaction, or a single environmental factor. But when it comes to understanding the origins of our complex, multilayered, and individualized happiness, this approach can be limiting. Rather, it's helpful to think of positive affect as a unique fusion of many emotions and behaviors, much as a symphony orchestra's sound comes from the synthesis of many instruments. If we were to hear the piccolo or bassoon or French horn alone, none of us could identify Beethoven's Fifth Symphony, let alone be moved by it.

In this book you'll discover the nine components of the symphony of Brilliant Health and how they come together in your body. You'll learn how to:

- Bring your most beneficial thoughts and behaviors to bear on your health and change the pathways and functioning of your brain.

- Take control of your health and your life by triumphing over the "victim brain."

- Envision your joys and passions and tell vibrant stories about them.

• Do the things you love, regardless of pressures to the contrary.

• Convert the sadness, fear, anger, and despair of trauma and illness into meaning, opportunity, and action.

• Create hope and resilience by using your higher brain to create new possibilities.

• Value your life and your body, and express heartfelt appreciation to others.

• Participate in the Marketplace of Giving.

• Tell the truth to yourself and to others.

Ongoing medical studies show that embracing this system can alter your biochemistry by reducing stress-related cortisol and enhancing IgA, a disease-fighting antibody and an essential component of healthy immune systems. A recent study we conducted, in conjunction with the Mayo Clinic and the National Research Center, shows how the Brilliant Health system strongly correlates with two important heralds of better health outcomes: perceived high quality of life and perceived emotional well-being. The same study showed these behaviors are powerful alone, and they are highly synergistic with one another.

For ten years we've been developing and perfecting simple ways to help people of all backgrounds put this system into practice. We've trained more than ten thousand people and witnessed dramatic results: from patients with cancer and advanced multiple sclerosis to physicians suffering burnout; from female executives enduring a work/no life imbalance, to re-tired Midwestern farmers in the midst of a postwork identity crisis. The system has worked because it uses each individual's unique strengths, rather than a one-size-fits-all formula.

It's been immensely rewarding for us to watch people's lives transform. Not only have they achieved better health, they have a more profound and richer life. Now it's your turn.

How Does Brilliant Health Work?

Envision standing on a never-ending spiral staircase. Your thoughts, emotions, and behaviors fuel your movement either upward or downward. Your climb toward better health be-gins with any one of the nine practices. Each can create al-terations in your body's biochemical environment, and all correlate with a variety of health benefits. Not only are you creating a healthier body, you're also building a heightened sense of competence and personal control. This healthy state, in mind and body, increases your feelings of happiness and exhilaration, empowering you to continue using the nine be-haviors as you climb higher. The best news: all of these prac-tices are completely within your control. You can *choose* to move upward toward Brilliant Health or live in negative emotions and tumble downward.

Why Is It Brilliant?

First, when we embrace this system, we shine with the brilliance of radiant health. Second, it's brilliant because we engage our maximum intelligence and emotional wisdom through choices that elevate us both mentally and physically, even in the face of illness or disability. In essence, we bring brilliance to our body.

Brilliant Health doesn't promise a disease-free, pain-free, un-aging life. Let's face it; sooner or later health and age-related issues will visit all of us. But whether we're in mint physical condition or facing a disability or a significant, even terminal, health issue, Brilliant Health brings us the highest possible emotional and physical quality of life.

Doin' What Comes Naturally

There's a deeper reason these nine practices work. They're tied to the historical evolution of human beings. We receive physiological rewards for engaging in the Brilliant Health practices because each of them supports the success and survival of our small-group, relationship-building species. At their most basic level, all of these practices make us resilient and adaptive as individuals. As a group of humans, this same resilience and adaptability allow our communities to thrive. And we need to feel part of a community to feel most alive and healthy.

For example, truth-telling, one of the nine practices, is the foundation for human society simply because without it, no social institution (whether it be a family, a circle of friends, or an organization) can succeed over the long term. When trust is destroyed, camaraderie collapses and progress ceases. It's no wonder then, that our bodies reward us for truth-telling and punish us severely for lying and deception. When we don't tell the truth, a polygraph clearly shows unhealthy increases in respiration, heart rate, and blood pressure in most of us, and that's only in the short term.

What you are about to experience in this book is a system of practices that benefits you by supporting your health as an individual, as a participant in relationships, and as a contributing member of the human community.

How Brilliant Health Affects Our Bodies

YOUR PERSONAL WHEEL OF HEALTH

Brilliant Health recognizes the natural complexity of health and what supports it uniquely in each of us. Our current state of health may result from many things. Genetics, age, nutrition, exercise, behavior, emotional and mental states, community ties, season, exposure to infection, and chemicals all play a part. To add further complexity, almost all of these factors are moving targets that change over time.

It's impossible to declare with authority the exact contribution of each factor in any illness. Consider a person with cystic fibrosis. No amount of positive emotion is going to suddenly generate the missing genetic material that causes the illness. But, as we've pointed out, the degree to which this person chooses to engage in the Brilliant Health practices can have an impact on how often he gets sick, how effectively the intact portions of the immune system respond, and perhaps, longevity.

Meet Ellen, our first shining example of someone who capitalizes on Brilliant Health.

Ellen is sixty-three, very active, eats well, and has never smoked. She has an unusual genetic disease known as familial high cholesterol, which leads to unfairly high cholesterol for her lifestyle and also led to the early deaths of her father and aunt from heart attacks. She has a fulfilling career and strong family and community ties. Ellen uses the Brilliant Health practices in many ways. She learns new ways of living effectively with her illness, volunteers at the local heart association, actively appreciates the wonderful parts of her life, doesn't blame, sets her intention to be happy, and does not see herself as a victim of her disease. Thus, in spite of her illness, she is ascending the spiral staircase. Her Wheel of Health may look like:

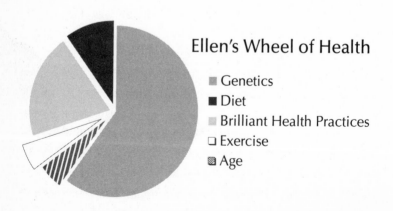

Ellen's Wheel of Health

- Genetics
- Diet
- Brilliant Health Practices
- Exercise
- Age

There is a significant genetic component to Ellen's illness, encompassing more than 60 percent of her health wheel. She can't change her genetics, but she can make an impact on them by choosing a Brilliantly Healthy life. In fact, the 20 percent of Ellen's wheel representing the Brilliant Health practices exerts far more than a 20 percent share of Ellen's experience of healthfulness. Her sense of vibrancy and emotional well-being spills over, motivating her to continue her low-fat diet, adhere to medications, walk daily, volunteer, and avoid smoking. In the end, she loves the life and community she has created, takes very few sick days, and has lived without evidence of heart disease far beyond her doctor's expectations.

In this book, you'll meet real people like Ellen, many with inspiring stories of how they implemented the nine practices. All of these people chose to engage in behaviors, thoughts, and actions that generated the positive emotions that brought them to their most happy and healthy selves.

For you, Brilliant Health practices may start out as a 90 percent slice of your health wheel, or it may be 5 percent. But you will never know how far they will change the composition of your wheel until you try.

Why Brilliant Health Now? The Evolution of Medicine

Why has it taken so long to explore the immense benefits of positive emotion? To answer that question, we need to take a brief journey into our species' health history, when infectious disease was on the rampage, causing the vast majority of death and disability. A quick glance back to only a hundred years ago shows the top causes of death in the United States were pneumonia and flu (20 million died in the 1918 Spanish flu pandemic), tuberculosis, and diarrheal illness.

So we fought back, developing antibiotics, vaccines, and antivirals. Huge strides were made in chemistry, physics, and biology to understand the underpinnings of those viral and bacterial illnesses. All told, we created a system of medicine focused on reactive, rapid, and acute care of infectious disease. It was quite an accomplishment, and, though the race isn't won (newly emerging viruses and prions, like those causing mad cow disease, still threaten), it's amazing to consider that the bubonic plague of the Middle Ages that killed a quarter of the world's population is something medicine can easily treat today.

Fast-forward to 1942, when something new and distinctly different happened: the word *stress* first entered the medical lexicon as a way to refer to something purely psychological that also had profound physical effects. Stress was not a disease, nor was it infectious, yet it had markedly deleterious effects on our bodies. As opposed to our infection-riddled past, most of the post-1950s causes of death and disability are related to lifestyle, behavior, and stress-related illness. These days, the top three killers in the United States are heart disease, cancer, and cerebrovascular disease.

Yet we are still applying a system of medicine that was designed to fight acute illness to these new killers. Unfortunately, vaccines and antimicrobials are not the solution. So the cure isn't as straightforward as we might have thought and has provoked medicine to think about health and illness in entirely new ways.

Early on, medical professionals believed that the healthy opposite of stress and depression was simply the *lack* of stress and depression. Though anyone who has felt giddy after a giant belly laugh, the glow of holding a new baby, or the warmth of affection with a loved one knows this already, science is starting to see that a state exists at the opposite end of the emotional continuum, something for which our species is preprogrammed: happiness.

Just as *stress* was once a new term in medical terminology, *happiness* is the new frontier of serious medical study. To show you how new this is, a search of the largest medical and scientific journal database produced over 700,000 articles on stress, depression, and negative affect, with a mere 4,000 pieces on topics like happiness, joy, and positive affect. Of those, more than 3,000 are from the last decade alone. We're just beginning.

Choosing Brilliant Health is the result of work we started thirteen years ago. When we began our study of happiness, we found it was hard to get others to take our work seriously. Even our closest friends and colleagues thought we were crazy. Publishers didn't want a book with *happiness* in the title. Even though people loved our model of happiness, we were asked not to use the *H* word in our keynote speeches. To most people, it implied a superficial denial of life's realities. Businesses and universities, in particular, didn't see *happiness* as a professional topic, and it made most scientists squeamish.

Today the field of positive psychology is thriving, new research on positive emotions is being aggressively funded, and mainstream media are running headlines about the connection between happiness and health. Harvard University offers a course on positive psychology that has become its best-attended class. The University of Pennsylvania's Positive Psychology Center offers a master's degree in applying positive psychology as a therapeutic tool. The Mayo Medical School recently offered a section on happiness (taught by Greg Hicks, coauthor of this book), and Claremont College in Southern California has a doctoral program in what makes people happy. Two hundred other colleges provide classes in well-being and happiness. And the two of us teach the Brilliant Health model to some of the biggest corporations and hospitals in the United States.

The Creation of the Brilliant Health System

OUR STORY

It all began with a simple idea. We wanted to improve our lives. So we decided to interview the five happiest people we knew. What those first five said was so intriguing we made what felt like a daring decision: to set out on an ambitious and ultimately exhilarating three-year journey to interview profoundly happy people all over the world. *What a great idea for a book,* we thought. *Happiness secrets from world cultures! How does someone create happiness in Istanbul? In Kyoto? In Buenos Aires?*

We crisscrossed the United States, from St. Helena, California, to St. Petersburg, Florida, from Mendenhall, Mississippi, to Minneapolis, Minnesota. Eventually, we traveled to six continents, visiting villages and major cities alike. Our adventures brought us to the four corners of the world including remote places like the bustling town of Puigcerda high in the

Pyrenees, the far reaches of southwestern Australia at Esperance, and charming Zapajar on the central coast of Chile. All told, we missed only Antarctica.

Each time we pulled into a new town, we'd wander through the streets, duck into cafés and pool halls, and ask the locals, "Who's the happiest person you know?" It never took them long to answer. We'd get the happy person's phone number, invite ourselves over, and often spend most of the day learning about him or her. Without the goal of proving a particular theory, we didn't go into our interviews with a research agenda or list of questions. We just let them talk. To our surprise, no one ever turned us away.

Meeting wonderful people, hearing amazing things, and having an adventure of a lifetime was thrilling. But there was one big problem. As we collected stories, we began to realize that not only would our book of happiness secrets never sell, it should never exist. For as diverse as the people were in every way, the stories they told us, at their core, were all the same story. Nearly everyone we spoke with had made the same set of intrinsic choices to be happy.

Thus began an intellectually meandering, stumbling-in-the-dark phase of our journey. To this day, our medical colleagues politely refer to our approach as an "emergent methodology." We call it "going with the flow." But "going with the flow" wasn't as smooth as it sounds. There were so many abrupt course changes along the way.

Course change #1: Rather than a collection of diverse stories, we recognized and then codified a model of the nine choices universally made by these people who seemed to have life wired regardless of their circumstances. Based on the model, we wrote a book called *How We Choose to Be Happy*, which went on to be translated into sixteen languages and became a national bestseller. Capturing the collective wisdom of individuals from around the world also gave us a new career. We began giving keynote speeches and conducting trainings on how to integrate the nine choices into life, how to use them to become better leaders, and how to use them to build better team cultures.

Course change #2 literally dropped at our feet. In 1999 we presented our happiness model, under the auspices of the American Hospital Association, to an audience of doctors in leadership roles. Minutes after we finished the presentation, something began to happen. We found ourselves cornered at the hors d'oeuvres table, in hallways, and even in the parking lot, as doctors pulled us aside to propose an idea. In one way or another, what they said was, "This model goes far beyond happiness and leadership. You've just presented the behaviors of my most successful patients."

That night, two fascinating and inspiring pieces of our intellectual puzzle dovetailed perfectly. The fact that doctors were so emphatic about the juncture of happiness and health, and that they saw a distinct relationship between our happiness model and wellness, sent us careening into an entirely new arena: medicine.

Of course, we began doing what we loved to do most: interviewing. We started by tapping into the incredible brainpower and experience of the medical professionals enrolled in the Health Research and Educational Trust fellowship programs, in which we are faculty. These advanced doctors and nurses run cardiovascular facilities, "Healthy Communities" initiatives, and patient safety programs. And since then, many others from around the world have lent validity to the profound relationship of the nine practices outlined in this book to positive health outcomes.

We continue to gather more data all the time. We're also working with practitioners in integrative medicine researching the influence of positive affect on mind/body interactions. Besides training doctors and nurses at some of America's leading health organizations, we're been applying the nine practices of the model to create innovative programs, like the Happy Heart Campaign for Mayo Clinic's cardiac patients. In addition, we have half a dozen other research studies under way correlating the nine practices with the success of patients dealing with diabetes, heart disease, and other illnesses.

This surprising period in our professional lives also brought us to Dr. Jen Seda, whom we met at the Mayo Clinic, when participants in our training program were being tested for levels of stress-related hormones and immune factors. She is the perfect collaborator. Having spent years studying and designing research in the biochemical mechanisms of mind-body communication, she's been an invaluable resource, providing us with a rich comprehension of the interaction of behavior, thought, and physiology. Jen has enriched this book with many of her own ideas, as well as fact-checked it for medical accuracy.

Throughout our world travels, we've been particularly fascinated by the impact of worldwide cultural mind-sets on happiness and, by extension, on health. Our unforgettable interactions at Baragwanath Hospital, an enormous medical complex bordering Soweto, South Africa, stand as being among our most heartbreaking yet inspirational experiences. Before launching our first day of training, we posed a question to the thirty-five medical professionals from eleven tribal groups battling that country's overwhelming AIDS epidemic: "In spite of their short life expectancies, what are the characteristics of your HIV patients who thrive?"

Even in a place so far removed from our own, the group articulated what were essentially the same nine practices outlined in this book. Although they may have used different vocabulary, their descriptions confirmed that this discrete grouping of practices positively affect health, even in the most diverse cultures.

While we have enjoyed and been challenged by our work with medical professionals, its most rewarding aspect has been the opportunity for the two of us to teach the nine practices directly to patients. Critically ill people, as well as those suffering from drug and alcohol addictions, are participating in our Brilliant Health workshops. The results have been stunning. Even those who have battled disease for decades and have tried countless other approaches report having made significant and immediate progress toward becoming emotionally and physically healthier.

We don't have a finish line. Each day we learn more about happiness, health, and the vital relationship between the two. Whenever we have an opportunity to talk with a social worker about the value of support systems, talk to a physician about the importance of patient attitude to recovery, or turn a random encounter with a stranger into an interview, we take it.

So the seemingly simple idea of studying happiness has blossomed into much more than we ever thought. It has not only become the basis of our training and consulting but also the foundation of the way we choose to live each day and the way we manage our own health.

OUR INTENTION

In writing this book, we strove to be inclusive of everyone, excluding no illness, syndrome, or disability, while tackling a topic that binds us as a human family—the desire to be healthy and live better. Our intention was to break down something as vast, complex, and important as positive emotions and offer you a tangible and practical road map to create them for yourself. And we wanted to make it all easily implemented by you whether you've got a serious illness or are already in the pink and want to do your best to stay that way.

To help you do that, we've designed exercises that you'll find in boxes throughout each chapter. There's also a questionnaire in Appendix 1, "Your Brilliant Health Quotient," that will help you create a portrait to see what you're already doing and where you might want to increase your efforts. You can take it now as preparation for reading the book, or you can take it at the end once you're fully fluent in the Brilliant Health practices.

Our hope is that you will embrace Brilliant Health and enjoy its benefits. Most of all, we wish for you a richer, happier, and healthier way of living. Life can be so good!

PART TWO

The Nine Practices

ONE

Intention

My thoughts freely flower,
My thoughts give me power.
No scholar can map them,
No hunter can trap them,
No man can deny:
Die Gedanken sind frei! (Thoughts Are Free)

—GERMAN FOLK SONG, composer unknown

Your climb up the staircase starts with Brilliant Health Intentions, an exquisitely powerful way to give your body a new and improved set of operating instructions. Intention has been a hot topic lately, and there's little agreement. Some people describe it as an "energy field" that binds us all. To others, it's what you do to look on the bright side. Yet others see it as a way to achieve material desires and a foolproof cure for illness, one that trumps genetics, environment, and personal health history. A Brilliant Health Intention is different. It's a powerful message we give ourselves, creating the positive emotions that propel us upward on the spiral staircase to good health.

Creating a Brilliant Health Intention happens at the moment you make a conscious choice toward your most beneficial thought, feeling, or behavior. In doing so you are purposefully giving yourself messages about who you want to be, how you want to react, and what actions you want to take. When we invoke Brilliant Health Intentions we have a deep sense of internal control and well-being because we're taking charge of our bodies, biochemistries, and, most specifically, our brains.

Though we may not realize it, most of us already use the power of Intention to invoke healthy physical responses. Virtually all of us have experienced the symptoms of a common cold coming on and used our intentional inner voice to say, "Not now!" thus initiating a complex immune response that wards off the virus. Some of us have dampened pain, calmed our digestion, quelled panic, overridden fear, and created alertness. We may have slowed our heart rate, lowered our blood pressure, and turned down our stress response.

With wondrous results like these, Intention may feel magical, but it isn't wizardry. It's tangible. At any moment you can take the opportunity to become aware of your thoughts, feelings, and behaviors and then consciously choose new ones. When you do, you're capitalizing on a basic truth: you can't always choose your circumstances, but you can always intentionally choose your attitudes and reactions. The key is that you're the one making the choice!

This chapter will give you practical instructions for how you can use something you've always possessed: the amazing power to intentionally create your own physical, emotional, and behavioral responses. In fact, your health is extremely well-served if you look at intention-setting as an indelible human right. But before we show you how to use intention-setting to achieve Brilliant Health, we want to paint a picture of just how profoundly your intentions can influence your mental, emotional, and physical well-being.

The Chemical Reaction

Conscious intentions are so important because you, and every human being, have access to a remarkable, naturally occurring chain reaction. It starts with your unique ability to shape your own thoughts. Your thoughts, in turn, have the power to influence almost every cell in your body. To explore this, let's take a short trip to our most complex organ, the brain.

No one fully understands every aspect of the brain, but we do know that our nervous system—the brain, spinal cord, and nerves throughout the body—forms a massive communications network of electric impulses and chemical messengers. The brain is our central processor, at all times both gathering information about our body and sending out instructions.

Each second, every organ, muscle, and inch of skin is relaying to the brain what is going on. The brain uses this information to decide what actions to take and gives mandates back to every organ. For example, it might help mobilize the immune system's army to quell an infection, demand a change in posture if a foot falls asleep, direct blood flow to the heart when we exercise, or focus on digestion after a meal.

All animals have a network of chemical and electrical communications that allows their brain to direct biological pathways throughout their bodies. But, unlike any other animal, we have more control over them.

How? Through consciousness, analysis, and active thought. These are all evolutionarily newer brain functions, also referred to as the higher brain. The lower brain, on the other hand, controls automatic reactions and activities, like heartbeat, breathing, and even rudimentary emotions. So while the higher brain enables choice, the lower brain supplies reactivity. Unlike a reptile that only has a primitive, lower brain that makes it instinctively freeze, attack, or run away from a threat in fear, we have the additional capabilities to lift ourselves into our higher brains and be rational, solve problems, and choose our responses intentionally. Since most of what we fear won't actually kill us, we have the luxury of time and the gift of consciousness to set our intentions, thereby determining our most helpful reactions to something we may initially experience as threatening.

Here's the most exciting news when it comes to your adult brain: new scientific data explains why Brilliant Health Intentions have such impact. It had been a long-standing belief among neuroscientists that the adult brain is unchanging, hardwired, and set in its function and form. So once we reach adulthood, they thought, we were stuck with what we had. In fact, just a few years ago medical students were taught that our personalities were etched in stone by age twenty-five.

But in the past few years a radically different picture has emerged. We now know that the adult brain has neuroplasticity, which means that it has the ability to change its structure and function in response to our experiences and thoughts. Though it often appears that the neural pathways have become hardwired, it's only because we're entrenched in certain patterns of thinking, and these become stronger with continual use. But just because many people don't choose to change doesn't mean we can't.

Opening New Pathways in Your Brain

When you set a Brilliant Health Intention, you marshal the capacity of your higher brain, reinforcing existing healthy neural pathways and actually building new ones. You direct yourself to a healthy physical and behavioral response, rather than an unhealthy or even self-destructive one. By repeatedly setting positive intentions like looking for joy or appreciating family members rather than being frustrated by them, you set up and strengthen new neural pathways to allow these healthy choices to become automatic or default settings. This becomes a self-rewarding, self-building cycle that continually propels you up the spiral staircase of Brilliant Health.

To help understand this, envision an irrigation system in which there are many furrows, though we've used primarily one furrow to deliver water for many years. This furrow grows deeper and deeper and, as a result of its constant use, it becomes the preferred delivery route for the water. But only one delivery route leaves the other furrows dry and robs most of the field of much needed water. To build new pathways for the water we have to clear the other furrows of rocks, debris, and dust, and use them repeatedly to make them deeper and increase their delivery capacity. A field with multiple furrows, all delivering water, is more productive, fertile, and more beautiful. Just as the health of the field improves, so will your life, as you repeatedly use Brilliant Health Intentions to deepen new attitudinal and behavioral pathways in your brain.

The power is yours. For example, if you've been only using one pathway to deal with issues and that pathway is an angry one, it's no surprise you feel angry much of the time. The same is true of any of the negative emotions. To change this you activate the three families of Intention.

How to Use the Three Families of Intention

We hope that you are convinced of the power of Intention and can't wait to roll up your sleeves and learn how to do it. There are three types of Brilliant Health Intentions: *In-the-Moment Intentions* that help us determine our reactions to specific situations; *Daily Intentions* that help us proactively set the course of each day; and *Core Intentions* that give healthy, ethical, intellectual shape to our entire life.

After well over a decade of teaching workshops, and lots of trial and error, we've learned what works best when it comes to making the practice of intentions concrete, practical, and easy. Once you've seen the impact of Brilliant Health Intentions on your body and how good you feel when you get the hang of it, you may become an intention addict.

In-the-Moment Intentions: The Anytime, Anywhere Stress Reducer

In-the-Moment Intentions are created in that split second between stimulus and response. They happen at the tiny yet precious deciding point when you first recognize a negative reaction, or an impending one, and then make a better choice that will guide you toward a healthier outcome.

You have the wonderful opportunity to set a Brilliant Health Intention every time life throws something unexpected, irritating, infuriating, scary, or disappointing in your path.

Here's how you do it: rather than respond reflexively, before any event of the day or when you first feel stress or anxiety, you immediately ask yourself three questions:

- **"What's my attitude or behavior right now?"** (Perhaps the answer is "Hostility, and I'm just about to start an argument.")

- **"Is this the most beneficial attitude or behavior?"** (The answer is probably "No.")

- **"Is there a more beneficial attitude or behavior I can choose?"** (The answers to this last question may be something like "I intend to relax, or be candid without blaming," or "I will show empathy," or "I will learn from the event.")

Then choose your best response. At this moment, you are in your higher brain. Stay there. Because of its neuroplasticity, you are encouraging your brain to deepen a healthy neural pathway or create a new one.

Once again, the most important point is, you're the one making the choice. You aren't on automatic pilot, merely reacting to what life throws your way. And you're not having a knee-jerk reaction to someone else. You're using the best of your brain's capacity to invoke positive emotions.

All day long, you can ask yourself the three questions listed above. When you do, you might, for example, decide to let go and allow a rudeness to have as little impact as water on a duck's back. Rather than grind your teeth about the traffic, you might decide to enjoy your favorite music, think about an exciting upcoming event, or phone a friend. When you find yourself in a defensive conversation, rather than the automatic response of defending yourself, you might set your intention to just listen. By far, our bodies prefer all of these newer, more positive intentional choices.

Let's take a relatively simple, short-term stressful situation to which we can all relate and then reveal the magnitude of negative effects it's actually having on the body.

CHOICE AT 33,000 FEET

You're on an airplane flying at 33,000 feet. The airline canceled your original flight so you're already three hours late to a much-anticipated family reunion. After standing in a security line that extended outside the front door, airport agents confiscated your new, expensive skin lotion. Angry and flustered, you get on board, only to find yourself jammed into a middle seat. Your automatic responses begin to spiral down, piling on stress about missing the reunion, fighting the traffic when you arrive, and the sheer incompetence of the airline.

The situation may be short-lived, but the physical impact is profound. As you obsessively check your wristwatch and look for every potential new delay, your leg is shaking, your heart is racing, your blood pressure goes up, your breathing is shallow and rapid, and you've got tension in your back and shoulders. Welcome to the realm of your reactive lower brain and its far-reaching physical effects.

You may or may not be aware of these profound physical reactions, but there are even more effects. Blood is being shunted to your muscles and heart, your immune system is ramping up inflammatory pathways and simultaneously decreasing viral and cancer surveillance; your body is preparing for fight or flight and thereby shutting down body functions like digestion and reproduction. It's also reducing blood flow to your brain's prefrontal lobes where planning and conscious problem solving take place. These defensive responses would be well and good if you were a caveman and there was a tiger to run away from or a hostile neighboring tribe to fight. But these are not healthy responses when sitting in an airplane seat for four hours, unless, of course, there's a tiger or a hostile tribesman sitting in the seat next to you.

The first step is to recognize that your unconscious intentions are triggering an internal voice that might be saying: "I don't have any control." "I have to give in to all these negative experiences." "I'm going to be tense and obsessive." Or, "I'm going to prove to myself just how miserable this flight can be." When we think bad things are happening to us over which we have no control, it triggers a feeling of helplessness. And the reason we become reactive is because we often don't realize we're slipping into this helpless place.

If the immediate physical effects weren't doing enough damage, there's more. When you're not choosing Brilliant Health Intentions, your unconscious mind can bring on the negative, and you create pathways in your brain that, indeed, reinforce the negative, painful, and threatening aspects of the experience. Your brain, now programmed to worry about a specific threat because of continued stress responses, starts to look for anything on the

plane that's wrong. It's taking its marching orders from your underlying conflict between feeling out of control and wanting to
be in control, which leaves you feeling victimized. This stacks
up to a confused set of unconscious intentions, which directs
you into the angry zone. Of course, none of this will help the
plane land any earlier.

Here's your Brilliant Health Intention moment! It is time
to set an intention to respond differently. It is in this moment
of awareness that you can take control of your flight experience and refocus on other reactions.

When this exact scenario unfolded for Shawna, one of our
students, she recognized she couldn't change her circumstances, but she could change her tense and angry reactions.
Since there were no hostile tribesmen in her row, she knew she
could set new intentions. After considering several possibilities, she intended to focus her thoughts only on being creative
for the rest of the flight. So how could she make the best use of
her creativity? She decided to write notes to each of the people
who were most special to her at the reunion. By the time she
landed, she'd produced fifteen notes with sentiments she'd always wanted to share with these people.

That first moment when Shawna made her choice to turn
to the positive, she took advantage of a uniquely human gift.
She leapt from lower reactive brain activity to the higher brain
functions, finding creative solutions, shifting her attention to
something self-affirming, and focusing on the real purpose of
the trip. Once her brain had been reprogrammed to focus on
the positive, it found other links to good, positive events. It's the
same effect that being in love evokes: everything smells, tastes,
and looks so much better.

Intention

Shawna walked off the plane feeling productive and inspired. Energized and calm, she was ready to enjoy the family party, or at least what was left of it. And, after an initial free fall down the spiral staircase, Shawna used intention to redirect upward.

The last time you were in a stressful situation that made you anxious, what were your conscious intentions? What might your unconscious intentions have been? In hindsight, what Brilliant Health Intentions could have helped you?

RAISING THE UNCONSCIOUS

Most of us are not used to thinking about intentions, and yet many of them are swirling around in our unconscious minds. But our intentions are still driving our actions, whether they're conscious or not. And that's why it's so important to bring intentions to the surface and then choose which of them to engage.

To live by intentions is a learned process, and it's unlikely that setting intentions will be a slam dunk when you first try it. Since it's a skill requiring awareness and practice, you need to keep at it until you have a success.

Fiona, one of the participants in our Brilliant Health workshops, knew she had to do something about her tension level. She was so tense that she was even tense about being so tense. Having just started working with us to be more intentional, she encountered something many of us have dreaded.

WISDOM AND WISDOM TEETH

While on her way to the oral surgeon for the extraction of her wisdom teeth, twenty-one-year-old Fiona felt anxious and fearful. Even though these reactions are completely normal, she knew they were bubbling up from her subconscious fears and they would not serve her well. So she pushed herself to shift her intentions as she walked into the office. As difficult as it was to switch gears, her new mind-set was to be curious and adventurous rather than stressed. She consciously focused all her attention on noticing the steps of the procedure, on the interactions of the staff and surgeon, and even on the beautiful orchids in the front office. As the appointment went on, she felt her anxiety begin to fade.

This is a victory of Fiona's conscious choice over an automatic response. She chose to put her attention on what made her curious rather than on what made her fearful. Fear is the most basic response designed to protect us from a threat, but by choosing to focus her attention on imagination and curiosity, she lessened the physical impact of that primal reaction.

Through our work with the Patient Safety Leadership Fellowship for medical professionals we've learned that the lack of clearly stated moment-to-moment intentions is often at the root of miscommunications and can even give rise to medically dangerous situations between doctors and patients. As a patient, setting your intentions before an appointment gives you the means to having the best interaction with your doctor. In response to being poked and prodded during the course of an examination, you can choose to listen, to respond honestly to questions, to not withhold information, to ask relevant questions, to partner with your doctor, and tell the doctor immediately when the information doesn't make sense. If these intentions are in play, the number of misdiagnoses and other medical mistakes that takes place would be radically reduced. Intentionality, alone, can make a big difference.

Identify an upcoming event that you feel might become tense, difficult, or unpleasant. What intentions can you set to guide you to how you will respond and how you want to feel during this interaction? Make the healthiest choices, remembering that what is most fun and pleasurable for you often generates the best physical response.

Even though moment-to-moment intentions take place in the tiny space between thought and action, from a neurological standpoint, they are crucial events. Recent brain research shows that even our simple intentions are not encoded in a single neuron. Intentions invoke an entire physical system that involves many parts of the brain. Our intentions are triggered in one area, actualized in connection with another, and get procedurally remembered in yet another location. What this means is the next time something happens, that complex neural pathway will be triggered again.

A single intention really keeps the neural pathways flowing. And that single intention can also, in an instant, make the difference between a rapid fall or upward climb on the Brilliant Health staircase.

Daily Intentions: Powering Up the Day

If you want to have a quick success with intentions, start by committing to a first-thing-in-the-morning Daily Intention. One of the reasons this practice works so well is because morning is the time when your body is most primed to receive instructions from your mind. As you awaken, your body's natural circadian rhythm creates a cortisol surge. This is its innate way of saying to your whole system, "Hey, this is important! Pay attention!"

By setting Daily Intentions, you can take advantage of your mind's readiness to accept new instructions and hold on to them throughout the day. Plus, first thing in the morning you haven't yet added the layers of mental clutter that build up during a day's activities. This is why a strong dose of Brilliant Health Daily Intention is a more powerful jump start to the day than a jolt of caffeine or sugary apple fritter. And it's a lot healthier.

Many of us have forgotten how much control we have over how our day will go. Brilliantly Healthy people are deeply aware of this fact and have created their own ritual for setting Daily Intentions, which are outcomes of two questions:

• How do I want to be today?

and . . .

• Throughout the entire day, where do I want to focus my attention?

In our workshops we find that Daily Intentions yield rapid and noticeable results. After a workshop, Bill, one of our participants, reported, "I'm addicted. Taking the time to frame up my day has changed everything. It's like a positive priming of the pump. On the mornings when things are too rushed and I skip my Daily Intention, there's an obvious difference in the way the day goes. How do I do it? I say them out loud, even though I live alone. It helps me keep the mental commitment and cements the intention, like planting a seed."

PRACTICING DAILY INTENTIONS

Like the individuals who craft them, Daily Intentions come in many forms, shapes, and colors. They're entirely individual, designed to meet our special needs and circumstances. We'd like to share some of our favorite Daily Intentions, gleaned from thousands of people in our workshops. They are compasses that guide us through the day and touchstones to which we can always return. But remember, the list below is only a suggestion of the numerous ways you can make your days happier, healthier, and more conscious. You should feel free to customize your own.

The Joy-Maker (Greg's Favorite)

"When I first open my eyes, I conjure up everything I'm looking forward to during the day and establish intentions about how I'll embrace each experience. For example, I intend to totally enjoy a lunch date with my son. I intend to walk to work, breathe deeply, and enjoy my surroundings along the way, rather than rush. I have the intention to be dynamic and connect with the people I'm working with during the day. The bottom line is, I create a feeling of excitement about what's coming my way. When I do this, I feel a happiness rush, and I have a guide to keep that happiness alive."

The Competence-Builder (Rick's Favorite)

"Because I travel so much, I have a chronic case of jet lag, which can be exhausting and hurt my ability to present to groups. I do my intention-setting every morning in the shower. 'Today I intend to be focused, relaxed, and energized. I intend to listen to my audience carefully. I intend to share everything I know that's relevant to the group. I intend to challenge them when necessary.' If I set my course in this way, I feel energized and capable throughout the day."

The Body-Booster

Augie is responsible for coordinating schedules at a large trucking company. It's a job full of nonstop pressure and crisis management. To arm himself with the mental and physical strength the job requires, he's developed an intention that works so well, he uses the same one every morning. In effect, it's a command to his body: *I have a strong and healthy body. I intend for it to work for me rather than against me.* "I say it, and I believe it. And my body reflects back to me that this is the truth."

The Esteem-Enhancer

Lori suffers from severe lower back pain. "I am most helped managing the pain by setting my focus at the beginning of the day. I stand in front of the mirror and appreciate my body rather than finding fault. I say out loud, 'Today I intend to be strong and stand upright, to breathe fully, to be alert, and to not allow pain to keep me from moving.' I intend to love my body for what it can give me, rather than expend more energy on pain or the things I don't like about myself."

The Movement-Motivator

At eighty-three, Esther is recovering from hip replacement surgery. "I have an intention every day to stay active. No matter how I feel in the morning, no matter how much pain and stiffness, I set my intention to get up and move. I intend to do all my favorite things rather than staying in bed. And I intend to not give in to the urge to watch TV or let the pain get the better of me. Having this message in my head helps me do just that."

> Customize your own Daily Intention and use it every morning within the first half hour after waking up for the coming week. Here's your chance to predetermine how you want your day to really go. It can be helpful to say out loud, "Today my intention is to . . ." Make sure you state an attitude or mind-set, not a specific goal or outcome.

The Team Approach

We've taught the concept of a Daily *Group* Intention to teams with whom we consult. One nursing group in a large medical center has started Daily Intention huddles before the morning shift. Here's how it works: Each team member takes a turn, and each stated intention is considered. Many of these intentions are embraced and become part of the group culture. For example, "I intend to do no harm, to listen to patients, to check my reports for errors, to focus on medication labels, to treat others with the highest respect." When twelve individuals state these intentions to one another, the entire chemistry of the group elevates. And it's interesting to note that this group has become one of the most desirable work placements in the medical center.

Intentions won't magically predetermine a day or, for that matter, a life that's clear sailing. It's not always the case that what you intend is what you get. Your days will have all sorts of surprises, some pleasant and some not. For the small disappointments, simply set new intentions. For those more troubling and threatening surprises, you'll learn a new technique in the Recasting chapter.

KEEPING YOUR DAILY INTENTIONS ALIVE ALL DAY

The toughest thing about engaging in any new behavior is figuring out how to keep it present and sustainable. Years of training and inadvertent practice have created neural connections in your brain that can jump directly to a pessimistic attitude when we try new behaviors. These beliefs and entrenched connections may be sabotaging your ability to change intentions by sending messages like "This is stupid," "It's not working," or "It's too uncomfortable."

You may have to find little mental tricks to talk to your brain. And once you get the hang if it, it's helpful to find ways to reinforce the Intentions you come up with. In our travels, people have come back to us with creative ways to remember their Intentions. We share these with the hope that one or more will speak to you:

• Use a Sharpie to write Intentions on the bathroom mirror so you see them alongside your reflection in the morning.

• Stick a Post-it note on your rearview mirror or the refrigerator door.

• Say your Intention out loud to yourself before you leave the house.

• Change your computer's screen saver every day to reflect your Intention for that day. (Kinetic memory kicks in when we're typing or writing.)

• Find an every-morning activity or ritual that triggers the impulse to carve out your Intention—when you pour your coffee, brush your teeth, take a shower.

• Involve an Intention partner and invite each other to state aloud your Daily Intentions.

Core Intentions: Aligning Your Mind, Body, and Values

Core Intentions are reflections of who we are at the fundamental level of values and morals and a portrait of who we most wish to be. With the focus on the big picture and the long term, these ongoing Intentions are guides for all the days of our lives and typically don't change much over time. They're strongly embedded in our identities, and, because they are so important to our basic operating systems, they form the rock-solid foundation from which our In-the-Moment and Daily Intentions grow. Though most of us operate from the bedrock of Core Intentions, many of us haven't formalized them into clearly articulated statements.

KEEPING YOURSELF IN PERSPECTIVE

Gerry, a high-level executive, says, "My Core Intentions are really lifelong Intentions, and, above all else, these four simple statements have repeatedly saved me from losing my sense of self:

- To have a strong relationship with my children.

- To honor my aging parents.

- To always tell the truth.

- To be kind.

"I have a deep feeling of security because I am so resolute in these intentions. I know they will drive everything I do. They direct every decision because they give me an anchor. With them as my guideposts, I experience joy, calm, and energy. I feel centered and so I don't get caught up in guilt, sadness, disappointment, and the loss of perspective that can happen in the get-ahead-at-all-costs environment at work."

For people like Gerry, Core Intentions are broad, operational statements that override all pressures to violate a sense of what's important and right.

Core Intentions often comprise the things we love, our values, ethics, and life priorities. The following are typical examples:

- To look for opportunities for new adventure.

- To contribute to the quality of the lives of others.

- To live light, unencumbered by "things."

- To tell the truth, be authentic, and not get caught up in drama.

- To accept myself and others.

- To search for wisdom.

- To keep my life organized.

- To keep constantly learning.

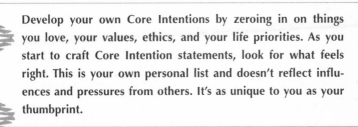

Develop your own Core Intentions by zeroing in on things you love, your values, ethics, and your life priorities. As you start to craft Core Intention statements, look for what feels right. This is your own personal list and doesn't reflect influences and pressures from others. It's as unique to you as your thumbprint.

As solid as our Core Intentions might be, when we're facing illness we're most vulnerable to losing sight of them. Because we become dependent on others and may feel weak, the Core Intentions of other people can take over. This injures us. We are forced out of a healthy alignment with our most deeply held beliefs and desires, and when we stress our systems in this way our bodies suffer at a critical time when they most need to be strong.

As if illness and the possible loss of Core Intentions were not troubling enough, this is the time when negative emotions are most likely to surface. Sometimes they can be so strong, they overwhelm our positive emotions. And among the strongest of these negative emotions is hate.

HATE AND YOUR FATE

Most of us are familiar with the visceral nature of hate. We have so many synonyms for it, words like *despise*, *detest*, and *loathe*, and all seem to connote our body's physical rejection of the thing we cannot stand to be near. We even say the things we hate make us sick. But because hatred is such an extreme and base emotion, it's all too easy for us to misdirect our hatred, to deceive ourselves with respect to who and what our enemies are. Meet Nancy.

INTENTIONS AND ILLNESS: A DECLARATION TO THE CORE

Nancy is a forty-four-year-old risk officer for a bank, with a husband and two teenage children. At the peak of her career, she was diagnosed with colorectal cancer that had spread to her pelvis and abdomen. When we talked with her at her home on a tree-lined street in Austin, Texas, we asked what she believed was the most helpful thing she did during her treatment. The key, she felt, was a change of intention.

Like many cancer patients, chemotherapy was part of her treatment regimen, and like almost all chemo patients, Nancy didn't look forward to the sessions. In fact, she hated them. But on some level, Nancy knew that she could not maintain her hatred without a cost. Already several weeks into the treatments, Nancy realized she needed an entirely new mind-set to create a healthier alignment with her treatment and to empower her recovery. "I had to make friends with the chemo because it was my lifeline," she says. "I couldn't hate or dread it." Nancy believes that each time she verbalized her intention to see chemo as helpful and good, it prompted a positive, powerful surge within her body that enabled her to more effectively fight her cancer.

Once she decided upon her new general intention of focusing not on an enemy but on healing, Nancy created a set of five additional Intentions that were a mix of attitudes and behaviors for the duration of the treatment. They were:

- To focus only on living.

- To see the treatments only as another appointment, just something to "add to my calendar."

- To go to work as much as she could.

- To actively appreciate the outpouring of love from others.

- To stay connected to important people in her life, even on days she didn't feel well.

For the lengthy duration of her chemotherapy and other medical procedures, Nancy told everyone about her Intentions. These Intentions, emphatically restated and therefore never forgotten through the long course of her cancer treatment, drove all of Nancy's decisions. She told her boss not to give her job away. She made it a practice to call a few friends each day. She wrote thank-you notes to all the people who had expressed their love and concern to her. She made sure to keep active in as many nonmedical parts of her life as was possible. And she showed up at work.

What's helpful about externalizing Intention statements is, by repeating them out loud to many people, we become accountable to them as they become ingrained statements of reality and an important part of every fiber and sinew of our conscious lives. Seven years after her diagnosis, Nancy is alive and well and continuing to set Intentions about her health, her kids, her new granddaughter, and her career.

> If you're dealing with an illness, regardless of its severity, set three to five Intentions that will be helpful in your decision making, your management of the disease, and your emotional reactions. Nancy's Intentions from the previous story can be a guide to creating your own, but, by all means, design Intentions to meet *your* specific needs.

To be accountable to her Intentions, Nancy stated them to everyone who would listen. Jason had his own unique way to keep his Intentions, and himself, alive.

LIVING LEGEND OR FORGOTTEN LEGACY?

At thirty, Jason felt indestructible. He emulated the lives of hard-drinking, hard-playing rock stars and their ilk, and he pushed himself to the limit. But when he felt a lump in his groin, he decided to check with his doctor. Medical tests revealed the lump was an aggressive melanoma. When Jason had first felt the lump, it was a marble-sized nodule, but it quickly grew to become the size of a golf ball and then, soon after, to the size of a fist. During the surgery to remove the growth, the doctors actually found five tumors, two of which were malignant and had spread into Jason's abdomen. Needless to say, Jason's prognosis was dire. He found himself facing the doctor and hearing the news that all of us dread hearing: "You have six to eight weeks to live," they told him. "You'd better get your things in order."

"I was completely naïve," says Jason of his approach to the news. "But I figured that I'd made myself sick, so I could make myself well. And, even though doctors hadn't given me the choice of living or dying, I just assumed I had that choice. The fight was on."

Just before he began his treatment, Jason decided on three Core Intentions to battle his illness:

- To never give up.

- To do every healthy thing suggested by his doctors.

- To take one day at a time.

Jason's medical team put him on a regimen of high-dose interferon treatments in addition to his radiation and chemotherapy. "The treatments made me so sick I was down to one hundred and forty pounds, and I was doubled over the toilet most of the day," he recalls. "I believe what kept me going, my savior, was a statement I had written in bold letters, laminated, and pasted on the floor right next to the toilet. As I was bent over the bowl vomiting, I tried not to take my eyes off that card. It said, 'I intend to do everything I can to live and be healthy so I can become a father, a husband, a hiker, a musician, and a composer.' I'm convinced my little handwritten card helped get me through those horrible months to where I am now." He believes these Intentions have also given his body the strength to survive long-term.

Fifteen years later we met up with Jason and also had the opportunity to meet his wife and two young sons. Over dinner at their home, he gave us his entire medical history and all that came afterward. The rock-and-roll days are over. He has become a founding owner of a high-tech company. In his free time, he's living his intentions. Jason's also a "hiker, musician, and a composer."

A cautionary note: Even though some of the true stories in this book seem miraculous, Brilliant Health is not about miracle cures. Not everyone with a dire diagnosis, even those with the strongest of intentions, will reach Jason's degree of success. With severe illness there are complex and hidden factors in play that make it impossible to offer guarantees. Our fundamental message is this: while there are always slices of our health wheel that we can't control, there are only good things to be gained from setting healthy Intentions and invoking any of the other Brilliant Health practices.

Uprooting Sabotaging Intentions

To be in Brilliant Health, it's important to examine preexisting intentions. Our underlying intentions about health come from many sources: our assumptions and beliefs about our bodies and our health, our family and cultural background, our feelings of self-worth, what our doctors tell us, and our expectations of life. Some of these are part of our conscious lives, which makes them easier to recognize, while others lie deeply embedded in our subconscious. Our bodies listen equally to both. The subconscious intentions are manifested as automatic behaviors and reactions we frequently don't even stop to consider, as if we installed a body-and-brain software program in childhood that we've long forgotten, but it's still running the show. And many of these overlearned beliefs may be hurting us.

Fundamental to the creation of Brilliant Health is bringing our unconscious intentions to light. For some people, psychotherapy is an excellent way to uncover these hidden intentions. We've also found, when asked the question, "What are your sabotaging intentions?" most people can, ultimately, access them. Once we become aware of them, like the software program, they can be reprogrammed. Here are some examples from our workshops:

SABOTAGING INTENTIONS	REPLACEMENT INTENTIONS
I don't deserve to be healthy.	To accept myself and appreciate my value.
To prove how smart I am by educating people about Crohn's disease.	To learn from others, especially from people in the Crohn's disease community.
Not waste time building relationships because people let me down anyway.	To look for positives in other people and appreciate them.
To expect perfection of myself and others.	To react differently than my mother did.
Being miserable is the only way I can express myself.	To talk about the good things that are happening.
To be well-liked by doctors and friends.	To be honest to doctors and friends.

Sabotaging intentions is like any other pattern, wearing hard-worn ruts of negativity in your brain. Years of training have made neural connections that jump directly to seeing the downside, to the threats, and to a pessimistic attitude. Go easy on yourself. Changing these long-standing behaviors is hardest at the beginning. You have to lift the wagon out of the ruts and start a new pioneering trail to happiness, creative thinking, and intentionality.

Ask yourself, "What are my sabotaging intentions? What under-lying beliefs do I have about myself that may be hurting me?" What usable replacement intentions would redirect your actions into a healthier realm?

We all know that "the path to hell is paved with good intentions." This is because we can set all the intentions we want and still, if we're not accountable to those intentions, we will begin an unhealthy descent on the spiral staircase.

Before you agree to do anything that might add even the smallest amount of stress to your life, ask yourself: What is my truest intention? Give yourself time to let a yes resound within you. When it's right, I guarantee that your entire body will feel it.

—OPRAH WINFREY (1954–)

TWO

Accountability

*The best years of your life are the ones in which you decide
your problems are your own. You don't blame them on your
mother, the ecology, or the President. You realize that you
control your own destiny.*

—ALBERT ELLIS (1913–2007)

Accountability may not sound like a lot of fun, but trust us, its
opposite is a lot less fun. When it comes to your health, Accountability fuels a joyful, courageous, and rapid climb up the
spiral staircase, while its absence precipitates a desperate free fall.

Over the last eight years, we've asked hundreds of doctors
and nurses if there's anything that seems to characterize which
patients will be *least* successful in recovering their health. Their
most common answer is, "They are the people who see themselves as victims."

We weren't surprised to hear that "victims" are poor healers, because we found, in our earlier research, that they're also
the least happy. After three years of searching out the happiest
among us, we set out to find their unhappy shadows. An odd
and overwhelming thing happens when you put out the word
you're looking for miserable people. The floodgates of misery

open. We were immediately deluged with calls from unhappy folk, eager to share their tales of woe. Their objective, it seemed, was to convince us that they were victims of unfortunate circumstances—bad breakups, lost jobs, and health problems, to name a few—all of which they felt had stripped them of any hope for a joyful or successful life.

Over the last eight years we also asked those same doctors and nurses about the other side of this question. "Which patients seem to have the greatest chance of being *most* successful?" Their answer was again nearly universal: "In spite of what's happening to these people, they see themselves as having personal power and control."

Once again, the medical professionals' conclusions were consistent with our happiness research. Ironically, many of the truly happy people we met had actually been victimized by traumatic events of far greater magnitude than our unhappy group, yet they refused to claim a "poor me" identity. In fact, they'd all made conscious, vigorous decisions not to blame themselves or others, sensing that chronic finger-pointing robbed them of the emotional capability and determination essential to living life to the fullest.

The second practice, Brilliant Health Accountability, means taking full ownership of your health and refusing to give away control of your life or fall into the traps of blame, victimhood, or apathy. We put our good intentions into action, allowing us to embrace what we can control rather than what we can't.

But before we dive into the practice of Accountability, we want to take you to the dark side.

The Blame Swamp

By force of habit and the impulse for self-preservation, sometimes we all sink into the swamp of blaming and victimhood. But as you'll see, these are silent killers that destroy our bodies and our sense of well-being. And their effects go beyond us as individuals. Blame is also a social disease, wounding relationships and entire communities. Its corrosive sound is: "It was so horrible, what she did to me," or, "It's all my family's fault I'm sick because we've got a history of diabetes," or, worst of all, self-blame: "I'm such a bad person for eating that entire chocolate cake." The terrible double whammy in this last statement positions you as both innocent victim of the alluring cake and guilty self-victimizer for having eaten it.

When we blame or feel victimized, we give away our power to whomever or whatever we blame, handing over control while rendering ourselves impotent. We give up ownership of our lives like royalty who abdicates the throne. It's physically impossible to feel the radiant joys of Brilliant Health—invigoration, competence, and fulfillment—while indulging in blaming at the same time. As opposed to authentic emotional reactions like sadness, anger, and fear, blame is a defensive stance that's a deep and murky swamp. When you stumble into it, you become mired and lose control over your own health.

Being a victim is not only harmful when you're dealing with illness, it can potentially determine who will get sick. In one of the largest longitudinal studies of its kind, British researchers studied more than ten thousand civil servants. It was discovered that those who believe they've been treated unfairly in life are far more likely to suffer heart attacks. Tracking initially healthy subjects for ten years, the study found that when compared to people who think their life is fair, the rate of cardiac events was 28 percent higher for those reporting even low levels of unfair treatment, 36 percent higher for those believing they'd experienced moderate unfairness, and 55 percent higher for those who felt they'd been subjected to the greatest amount of injustice.

This is not to say we're never victimized. In one way or another, we'll all be victims of social conditions, disease, discrimination, or family genetics, and at the receiving end of greed, revenge, and mean-spiritedness. But these realities are different from lowering ourselves into a state of perpetual victimhood. If you choose to frame yourself up as a victim, either in your own mind or in the way you represent yourself to others, you're creating an emotional wound that can transform into a physical one.

The Victim Brain

When we experience ourselves as chronic victims, we're creating an internal state equivalent to being under constant attack. Imagine a terrified rabbit the instant before being grabbed by a hawk's razor-sharp talons. It's paralyzed by fear, unable to move, and, in terms of active thinking, the rabbit's brain is entirely closed down. As humans, being a victim, or prey, shuts down creative ways of thinking, of finding options, alternatives, or solutions. We merely react to what we see as threats.

Nothing more abrasively ramps up our sympathetic nervous

system than constantly thinking about being under attack or being hurt, and responding as if danger lurks around every corner. Blood pressure and heart rate jump up, digestion shuts down, and the immune system prepares for battle.

When this becomes a way of life, we're stuck in the lower-brain functions of reacting, with a direct impact on brain regions that secrete chemicals into the bloodstream. When these chemicals are produced continually, they can negatively affect many organs. We eventually reach an exhaustion phase, the unhealthy endpoint of excessive stimulation from anger, fear, and anxiety. This results in a plunge down the Brilliant Health staircase into a potential host of undesirable outcomes: reduced sex drive, insomnia, depression, decreased memory, poor cognition, impaired digestion, and immune deregulation.

Even the biggest blamers and self-identified victims want to have good sex, sleep well, think clearly, and remember where they've been. And most important, who doesn't want their immune, digestive, cardiac, and endocrine systems to function properly?

We've noticed in our Brilliant Health workshops it is only when we describe the damage blame can wreak on the body that people start to really assess their own levels of defensive blaming behavior. Once you understand how much your victim brain is hurting you both emotionally and physically, you might be truly motivated to consider how to leave the blame fest and go to the health fair.

Think of a stressful issue for which you blame another person or group. First, write a description of the situation and people involved. Next, write for five minutes about how you feel hurt, who did this to you, what they did, and what they need to do to make it right. Notice how your body is reacting. Now, write for five minutes about your part of this situation—what you have done to create the situation, and what you can do to change it. The ultimate power is in your hands. The past is done, so what can you do from this point on? Notice how you feel now: energize, empowered, capable?

It's not always easy to change behavioral patterns, but potentially it is a life or death decision. If we still haven't convinced you about blame's dire consequences, maybe Heidi can.

FROM THE HEART : IMPRESSIONS OF A TRANSPLANT NURSE

Heidi has worked in the volatile world of heart transplant medicine for more than twenty years at a medical center in the Deep South. Her observations of patients in this high-risk field give us dramatic case histories of the impact of accountability.

"The patients who do best ask, 'To get better, what do *I* need to do today?' The unsuccessful ones say, 'What are *you* going to do to me today?' This last group are the patients who keep coming back with problems postsurgery and have more frequent incidents of organ rejection."

Heidi told us the story of two young female patients who exemplify the extremes. Both came to the health center after collapsing with what was later diagnosed as heart failure due to rare cardiomyopathies. Both were comatose when they arrived at the hospital. Only adding to their already taxed cardiovascular systems, they were both smokers, overweight, and had high cholesterol and blood pressure.

That's where their stories diverge. When Ashley awoke, she was angry and stayed bitter and resentful for the five months she remained in the hospital waiting for a properly matched heart donor. She complained constantly to Heidi and her colleagues about her care, her unfair genetics, her substandard doctors, and wallowed in self-pity, deeming every setback the hospital's fault.

On the other hand, Paige emerged knowing she needed to change. This was her wake-up call. "Today is a new day, I am in charge, and I will do everything I can to get back into the world." Given that she had no choice but to reside in the hospital, her most forceful intention was to maximize the control she did have. She built relationships with Heidi and the nursing staff, befriended and encouraged other patients, and never missed a meeting of the patient support group. She began a program to give up smoking, learned to make healthy nutritional choices, adhered to her medications, and actively created an intention to support and love her body. Though she felt the same initial grief, terror, and sense of unfairness as Ashley, she acknowledged those feelings but knew she had to let go of them to get better.

Though Ashley and Paige were matched physically, Ashley remained extremely negative and was in a chronically agitated emotional state. She continued sneaking cigarettes and refused to adhere to a healthy diet and medications. For all these reasons, the medical center ultimately judged Ashley to be a poor prospect for a transplant procedure and moved her to a neighboring hospital that was willing to take on her case.

On the other hand, Paige remained committed to healthy

changes in her lifestyle and continued as a resident of Heidi's hospital. She received a new heart eight months after her admittance. She suffered no rejection, continued to use the hospital's outpatient facility for routine exams, and returned only once four years later for medical tests. Now in her early forties, rather than giving herself a birthday party each year, she throws a bash to celebrate the anniversary of her new heart.

The medical center that took in Ashley found a perfectly matched heart nine months after her initial collapse. Sadly, she died on the operating table of hyperacute organ rejection. She was thirty years old.

The victim swamp may have been instrumental in sucking Ashley under. She refused to take any responsibility, subjecting her body to insults beyond the disease, like smoking, refusing medications, and poor diet. Her wheel of health also reflected the effect of her emotional state as she kept her stress hormones running on high. All these factors may have kept her immune system primed to look for the next attack. The type of rapid rejection that took her life is often due to preformed antibodies that lie in wait of the new, alien tissue. When the transplant heart was introduced to her body, her immune system detected it immediately and catastrophically rejected it.

Heidi summed it up best, "There's no way to know for sure how much positive emotions influenced either of the two outcomes. But ask any nurse in this unit, and they will tell you there's never an upside to being a victim. You doom yourself and your body to negative outcomes."

Are you sufficiently shocked by the effects of blame and victimhood and convinced that you want to avoid them? There *is* a Brilliantly Healthy alternative.

Achieving Accountability

If the "Victim's Lament" is, "Why me?" the accountable approach is, "What can I do about it?" Happiness, quality of life, and healing are the result of taking control. When we experience setbacks or, even worse, genuine disasters, there's a simple, powerful question we can ask ourselves: "What's *my* role?" The mere act of posing this question to ourselves delivers the only true sense of competence and satisfaction. And it leads to two very compelling follow-up questions.

- "What did I do to contribute to the problem?" or, "What might I have done differently?"

- "What can I do to make things better?" or, "What action can I take that will help me?"

When we ask ourselves, "What's my role?" we are not blaming ourselves but are engaging in a rigorously analytical and self-affirming step toward healing. By mentally stepping back and focusing on our role, we avoid the futile and energy-draining exercises of figuring out what others did to us, of wishing things were different, or of wanting other people to change. In fact, by focusing on ourselves consciously, we reaffirm our own power to change what's within our own sphere of control.

What has been your part in creating your current health condition or illness? What active part can you play in making your health better?

ACCOUNTABLE DOES NOT MEAN RESPONSIBLE

Accountability is not responsibility, which is doing what's expected and right. Responsible people pay the bills on time, put food on the table, and get themselves to work. When we're accountable, we have an ownership mind-set. The hallmarks of this mind-set are:

Determination: The self-motivating tenacity that overrides any obstacle and translates into attitudes like, "It's up to me!" and, "I can do it, and I won't give up," and, "I'm up for the challenge!"

Discipline: The commitment to act on our intentions and follow through. "I stay the course. I adhere to my treatment plan, my diet plan, my exercise regimen, and my other commitments to myself."

Nondefensiveness: The refusal to respond to people or situations defensively, because defenses only weaken our sense of self, distance us from other people, and drain energy from our bodies. Although it may seem counterintuitive, the more we defend ourselves using verbal attacks, passive-aggressiveness, or complete withdrawal, the weaker we become.

THE FIGHT IS ON

Yolanda is a teacher from Miami who comes from a vibrant and active Cuban-American family. Her relatives take a celebratory approach to life, and Yolanda had always embraced this culture with enthusiasm. For most of her life she indulged her passions: getting together with friends after work, spending her weekends sunning on the decks of the famous Art Deco hotels of South Beach, and treating herself to shopping and restaurant-hopping. She was always on the go. But ill health began to creep up on her. She often found herself too exhausted to do her favorite things anymore, and she couldn't find relief from debilitating joint pain.

Despite visits to a long succession of doctors, she couldn't seem to make progress against her pain. The physicians she consulted were unsure of Yolanda's diagnosis, yet they were willing to experiment with regimens of antidepressants, pain medications, and sleep aids. But each new prescription only made her feel worse. Chemically numb from a constellation of medications, Yolanda eventually found herself immobile in her beautiful home with what was finally diagnosed as fibromyalgia.

The once active, vibrant Yolanda withdrew into a defensive haze. She was frustrated by her physician's lack of solutions. And then, after being couchbound for an entire weekend, Yolanda hit the end of the line. She realized she'd watched a season's worth of back-to-back *Law & Order* episodes. Somehow this trivial milestone allowed Yolanda to reach the insight that she did not want to surrender to a slow withering away. And this sparked a desire to activate her last shred of energy. Instead of giving up and just living with it, Yolanda's desperation led to a decision in which she became accountable. "As of right now, this is not acceptable," she told herself. "I am no longer willing to live like this."

Yolanda vowed to keep investigating her condition until she found answers. "My mind-set was, I *can* solve this," she says. "Feeling better is not debatable. I am in control, not my disease, not my doctor—and there have to be answers out there for me."

Instead of continuing her *Law & Order* marathon, Yolanda started a Search for Health marathon, doing everything she could to free herself from the miasma of dizzying medications, deadening pain, and nonaccountability. Yolanda took a disciplined approach to networking with friends, sifting through online research about fibromyalgia, and reading voluminously.

Knowing that she had a non-life-threatening diagnosis and had not responded to the treatments prescribed by her doctors, she relentlessly investigated numerous options. After a series of wrong turns and dead-ends she finally found relief working with a naturopath and an acupuncturist. In retrospect, the pivotal moment came when *she* took control. Though 75 percent of her symptoms are gone, she continues to seek out alternatives for the remaining 25 percent.

Like Yolanda, we all have times we want to turn over the steering wheel to our doctors, our families, or our friends, yet that rarely gets us where we want to go. The truth is, we're in the driver's seat, whether we like it or not. And if we want to stay on the route to Brilliant Health, accountability requires that we grab hold of the wheel.

ACCOUNTABLE BRAINPOWER

The accountable brain is the "I'm in charge" brain. Research has shown us that pain is actually perceived as lessened when patients believe they have some control over it. Studies that look at areas of brain activation with MRI or PET scans have subjected patients to pain (usually a nondamaging heat source) while recording activation in different brain areas. When patients have influence over setting their own level of pain, they can tolerate increased temperatures. Having control seems to actually reduce activation in the brain's pain centers, even with increased objective levels of pain induction. It is highly likely that Yolanda's conscious feeling of being accountable, that is, owning her illness and being in control of her life, changed her perception of pain for the better.

Our Genetic Blueprint and the Fates

Even before the mapping of the human genome, the medical community had begun linking genetics to an increased risk for a wide variety of illnesses, like asthma, diabetes, heart disease, and depression. Unfortunately, many people saw this as an invitation to blame everything on our genes and, therefore, simultaneously believe they had no control over their health. Yet, for all of these diseases, our behaviors, thoughts, and emotions still play a large part in their severity, our symptoms, and our ability to recover or live with them.

GENETIC INGREDIENTS AND THE CHEF: TAVERN ON THE GREEN OR HELL'S KITCHEN?

How do genes work? Genes are the code for all proteins made by our bodies, and proteins determine nearly everything about how our bodies look, feel, and function. Not only are proteins the major building blocks, literally the structures that make up most of our cells, they are among the many messengers from one cell to another, directing blood flow traffic, running metabolism, digestion, reproduction, respiration, rebuilding, repair, immune activation, and almost everything else!

So, in essence, genes are the recipes for these proteins. But, they are *not* the chefs. We are the chefs because we create much of the biochemical environment in which our genes function through the combination of our life experiences, including everything we eat, everything we think, and everything we do. Because of this, we are instrumental in encouraging certain genes to express themselves while suppressing others.

While we may always have a genetic predisposition to high blood pressure or high cholesterol, we can exercise, eat healthfully, not smoke, take necessary medications, and implement the nine practices in the Brilliant Health model. Ascending the spiral staircase is the outcome of granting yourself the power to create the best possible conditions to support your own unique genetic design.

TWO CHEFS: TOM AND TINA

Tom and Tina represent two approaches regarding their respective genetically related health issues.

Tina's story typifies the *un*accountable approach. She weighs three hundred pounds, has trouble walking and breathing and, while she'd love to play with her young grandchildren, she doesn't have the stamina. Her poor eating habits, lack of exercise, and excess weight have led to high blood pressure and diabetes.

When we sat down to talk with her, she had a very wounded

response. "Everyone in my family is fat," she told us. "I inherited fat genes. I'm furious that I'm being robbed of my health."

There is hope for Tina, but focusing on a family genetic history she can't control will only generate negative emotions, including depression. It's true, most of us know someone who can eat anything and not gain a pound. It may not seem fair, but blame and envy don't help us choose a smaller portion of a healthy meal. They don't help us feel joy about our amazing bodies or motivate us to get off the couch and maximize our own personal biochemical makeup. Tina had no part in creating her genetics, but she could cook up a beneficial environment in which her genes operate.

The Fates have also been unkind to Tom's family. His male lineage has a genetic predisposition to early cardiac disease. His grandfathers, father, paternal uncle, and brother all died of heart attacks before the age of fifty-three. As long as Tom can remember, he assumed he'd have an abrupt and early death, so he was thrilled to celebrate his fifty-fifth birthday. Two days later, though, everything changed. He was rushed to the emergency room with severe chest pain. Tom thought it was the end, and it could have been. But, he turned the crisis into the beginning of a new and healthier life. Although he'd always worked out, followed a low-fat diet, and never smoked, this close call pushed him to look at every aspect of his life.

"I realized that stress was my Achilles' heel. 'To hell with our bad health history,' I thought. There's a lucky guy in every story. In this one, it was going to be me." A large source of his stress was in taking on more than he could realistically accomplish. This made it impossible for him to do anything well, which left him feeling anxious a great deal of the time. So he set his intention on doing excellent work by taking on one thing at a time. He learned to say no to more things. Now Tom's proud of the work he does and has more time to exercise and play sports, spend time with his family, and relish every moment.

Tom's convinced his attitude made the difference. "I have no doubt that attitude profoundly affects health. Being happy makes you do healthy things, and being healthy makes you even happier. If you're happy, you want to stick around, so you keep doing the healthy stuff. It's a cycle of well-being."

Tom's right. That fist-sized muscle, the heart, is sensitive to changes in our emotional state. It's particularly affected by stress and the attitude of being a victim. Taken together, those attributes mean that acutely stressful events, like a fight with a spouse or poor review on the job, get our heart pumping harder, and also elevate blood pressure. In more than one hundred studies involving more than 20,000 individuals, hostility and anger are shown to be independent risk factors for having a heart attack. New data indicates that these high-stress states (as well as depression) are associated with high levels of Il-6, an inflammatory immune protein, which may help create the biochemical environment triggering a heart attack. Other studies show that post–heart attack depression increases the risk of a second major cardiac event and reduces overall survival rates.

Maybe it's no surprise that four years later, Tom has not had a recurrence. Trim, productive, and enjoying life to the hilt, he's living proof that the genetic Fates can be persuaded by accountable behavior. Tom is *determined* to overcome the family blueprint, he's *disciplined* about his health program, and he doesn't succumb to any of the obvious *defenses*: self-pity, blaming, or cynicism.

> What's your family's genetic heritage? Do these genetics affect your health? To what degree can you override them? How?

Living on the far opposite end of the accountability continuum are the disquieting yet fascinating people who seem to be magnetically drawn to not healing. We have entered the realm of the Hungry Ghost.

The Realm of the Hungry Ghost

Aunt Ruth loves two things: being sick and complaining about it. Years ago, at the age of thirty, she convinced everyone she was at death's door. At eighty-two, she's still standing on the threshold. Why would anyone *want* to be sick? This is a question we hear repeatedly.

To answer the question, let's take a look into the realm of the Hungry Ghost. It's an image we borrow from Buddhism of a frightening apparition floating in the air in front of us. It has an enormous belly. Its legs and arms are withered, its neck the size of a straw, and its mouth the size of a pinhole. It is frantically hungry, but with that tiny mouth, it cannot be fed. Its power comes not from meeting its own desires but from its overwhelming neediness and deprivation. This is an apparition that rushes in only one direction on the health staircase: downward. And it tries to take everyone else down with it.

In practical terms, we are describing the *professional victim*, the victims of circumstance who gain their strength from not healing, from constantly complaining, and from rallying others to support their victim state.

We all carry some form of the ghost within. But even if we don't see ourselves as classic Hungry Ghosts, it's the more subtle forms of ghost-hood that we all have to monitor. We have to be honest with ourselves and ask, "Is there a part of me that is unconsciously sabotaging my own efforts to feel fully well? Am I attached to historical fears, family patterns, or social values that keep me from getting better? Am I punishing myself physically with guilt carried from the past? Could it be that I'm entrenched in negative expectations about my body, and almost loyal to my darkest symptoms, perceptions, and projections? Do I suffer from survivor's guilt?"

The happy ending to the story is that you can use your intellectual powers of self analysis, understanding, and creativity to bust the ghost. The first step is awareness that ghost-like behavior is getting in the way. Setting intentions to find new and healthier responses that don't entrench the Hungry Ghost within will guide you onto the path to de-haunting.

If you find this difficult, you may be dealing with deep-seated, subconscious issues or patterns. This is the perfect time to avail yourself of therapy or some other form of psychological self-exploration.

The Intelligence of the Beasts

In the entire animal kingdom, nonaccountability to self is a plague only among humans. Hawks don't ponder their aviation choices. They naturally soar on updrafts to preserve energy. If beavers could decide to party instead of building dams, they couldn't raise their young and be protected from predators. And lions don't make self-destructive decisions to lose sleep in favor of a late movie, and then sleep late when they should hunt. If you think about it, the natural order of things dictates that an unaccountable penguin will soon be a dead penguin.

When it comes to humans, the natural formulas for accountable behavior are often altered by civilized society. All the intellectual capacity in our magnificent brains comes with a price. It may give us the incredible ability to think consciously, but it also gives us the ability to override our naturally healthy selves and rationalize, lie, deny, avoid, retreat, and ultimately be completely irresponsible when it comes to making healthy decisions.

It's too bad that nonaccountable behavior is so trendy. We're titillated by the nonaccountable actor who behaves badly and ends up in rehab. We reward the politician who "apologizes" for dissolute behavior. And we're fascinated by the stereotypical self-destructive artist. But our bodies are far wiser. From the activation of the brain, to immune function, to digestion, to our heart, every cell responds to the positive emotions we create from within. Our bodies love the self-affirmation that comes with accountability.

Accountability leads us farther up the Brilliant Health staircase, and one of the most accountable things you can do for yourself is to identify and focus on your passions.

Take your life in your own hands and what happens? A terrible thing: no one to blame.

—ERICA JONG (1942–)

THREE

Identification

Everything you can imagine is real.

—PABLO PICASSO (1881–1973)

Imagine having an inventory of everything you love, a collection of your delights and your passions. You might have written it in a journal or spiral notebook or even on the back of a napkin. Regardless of the form, its invaluable beauty is that it describes the route to your most turned-on, elevated, and ideal state of being. It paints a self-portrait of you at your happiest and most healthy.

Our third practice is called Brilliant Health Identification, in which you bring to mind the things that give you joy. Identification involves three activities: discerning your passions and most significant life experiences, then envisioning them, and finally, telling stories about them. One of the most attractive things about the practice of Identification is that you can do it any time and in any place. And it's fun! You don't need anything but your imagination.

Have you ever noticed when you purposely think about something you love, or share a favorite story from your life, you start to feel better? Here's why: Just thinking about your passions evokes positive emotions that generate your own customized antidepressants. Chemicals like norepinephrine, serotonin, dopamine, endorphins, and oxytocin kick in, allowing for mental relaxation, reduced pain, and new psychological growth, all of which are the magnificent self-rewards that arise from just giving yourself the pleasure of visualizing joy.

Identifying Passions

Let's go on a thought-provoking and far-reaching journey to identify everything that brings you joy. Here's how:

BUILDING YOUR BLISS LIST

Your Bliss List is best described as a summary of your love-to-do's, rather than your have-to-do's. If you want an easy way to bring your passions to the forefront, take a few deep breaths and clear your mind. Don't think about your job or responsibilities at home. Set a timer for five minutes and begin to speed-write. This means to write as fast as you can without stopping. Focus on what thrilled you in the past, what activities you delight in now, and what would most excite you in the future. Think of little things like placing fresh-cut flowers in your home. Think of huge things like a yearlong stint in India studying Eastern culture. Then think of everything in between, like puttering in your garden, diving into a mystery novel, or a weekend ski trek with your family. Don't censor or judge. It's impossible to come up with a wrong answer unless, of course, you fall into the trap of listing what you think you should love (such as spending time with all your relatives). Indulge yourself in an act of sheer self-affirmation.

When the timer rings, take a moment to notice how you feel. In the years we've worked with groups of patients and corporate teams, this activity usually invokes palpable changes in the room's energy. For some, it's a feeling of lightness and joy, for others, deep thoughtfulness. A few find the experience frustrating, a kind of window shopping excursion filled with longing. Once you've done it, notice your own response and ask yourself, "How do I feel and why?"

Take a few more minutes to enhance your list by considering some additional questions:

- If I had an afternoon without obligations, how would I spend it?

- About what social issues or causes am I most passionate?

- Who are the people who energize me?

You're not quite done. Now that you've let your brain conjure these joys, it's time to turn to another source of intelligence.

SHARPENING YOUR BIQ: BODY INTELLIGENCE QUOTIENT

Though much of this book focuses on the impact of thought and positive emotion on your body, you can tap into an incredible reverse flow of information. By reading messages from your body rather than your mind, you can add to your Bliss List.

Our bodies are giving us important messages all the time, and they're never fooled by the shoulds. Think about the last time you felt the hair standing up on the back of your neck, a gut feeling, butterflies in your stomach, your heart in your throat, or feeling warm all over. Detecting and reading such sensations are core elements of your intuition. On a physical level, your body is continually registering millions of sensations and sending data to your brain, but only a small percentage gets through to the conscious level. When we push ourselves to become more aware of these messages, we take advantage of the great wisdom they offer.

If you want to use your body as a compass to what you love, notice when your body gives you a positive message, like a spread of warmth through your belly, a feeling of lightness, a glow, or a tingling. When they happen, stop, notice what you're doing in that moment, and write it down on your Bliss List.

You've finished your Bliss List for now. You've let your brain conjure your joys, and you've listened to messages from your body. But it is a work in progress. We recommend you carry the list with you for a month and continue to notice what brings you joy, adding to it all along the way.

With your Bliss List in hand, you're ready to go. The surprising thing is that you can move up the staircase of Brilliant Health without actually *doing* anything on the list.

Just Think About Your Passions

To your brain, just thinking about a passion is shockingly similar to actually doing it. Researchers have shown the same parts of the brain are activated whether we actually experience something or vividly imagine it. In other words, picturing an image of a tranquil beach activates the same area of the cerebral cortex as actually seeing a tranquil beach. Tasting the first bite of a deliciously sour lemon tart triggers the same area of the brain as does imagining that first mouth-puckering bite. Just thinking about getting under a warm flannel blanket on a cold night activates the same area of the brain as actually being wrapped up in it.

Vividly imagining sends messages to our limbic system (the feeling center of our brain), to the endocrine system (the control center for all our hormones), and to our autonomic nervous system (which controls functions like heart rate, blood pressure, perspiration, respiratory rate, and so on).

Think only about one of your greatest passions for three minutes. Note how you feel physically and emotionally afterward.

TREATING INSOMNIA WITH BLISS

The next time you wake up at three a.m. in a fit of overthinking, try an experiment. Rather than being consumed by stressful thoughts, direct them to your Bliss List, and let the positive images wash over you. We've found this technique often helps calm people, redirect stress, and allows them to get back to sleep more quickly.

Why does it work? The mere anticipation of stress can be as harmful to one's body as the actual experience. Stress, or the anticipation of it, releases cortisol and epinephrine, which send messages along the nerves that stimulate the heart, muscles, and digestion. You don't want to get revved up when you're trying to get back to sleep. Rather, the goal is peacefulness without an adrenaline rush, so pick something soothing from your Bliss List (like snuggling in front of a fire, walking in a forest, lying on a warm beach). Make sure you don't choose things that get your blood pumping (like snowboarding, Jet Skiing, or performing to a crowd).

When morning arrives and you first awaken, you have another opportunity to take control of your thoughts. Not only is it a good time to set your Daily Intention, it's also a time to focus on pleasure. Before negative thinking seduces you, direct yourself toward the anticipated joys of the day ahead: a stimulating project at work, your son's soccer game, the novel you can't seem to put down. In addition, conjure the qualities you treasure most about each of the favorite people you'll encounter that day: their humor, intelligence, thoughtfulness, warmth, and smiles. By setting these intentions, you're conditioning both your mind and body to capitalize on the joys ahead. Go ahead and make your mind a beautiful place to live.

DOUSING FLARES

Imagining bliss is an ideal way to deal with stress and stress-related disease. Beth, a twenty-two-year-old economics major, has suffered from occasional mild asthma for years. She's found that when stress at school or work begins to pile on and she feels her breathing begin to get tight, she relieves her symptoms by taking her medication and immediately conjuring the most calming image from her Bliss List: playing with her two dogs when they were puppies.

Diseases particularly susceptible to acute stress-related flare-ups, like asthma, allergies, inflammatory bowel disease, and migraines, respond very well to what we call Intensive Bliss Therapy in which you draw your attention to what's positive. In addition to dealing with stress, Bliss Lists can also help you deal with pain.

ON THE OTHER SIDE OF PAIN

At seventy-two, Gabriella has suffered from rheumatoid arthritis for almost forty years. With multiple joint replacements, she refers to herself as "Bionic Woman." After twelve surgeries, including wrist fusions and replacements of one hip and two knees, she lives in constant pain and can write with only her fourth and middle fingers.

"It's not that I don't wake up feeling lousy, even depressed sometimes. But when I do, I lie in bed and concentrate on the day ahead. I see myself swimming. I feel the warm water against my skin and the pleasure of soaking in the sauna. I see myself enjoying a good biography on the couch. Other people see me as disabled, but I see myself as high-functioning and healthy. It's simple, really. My morning mantra is, 'Get up. Happiness is waiting on the other side of this bed!' I truly believe that my mind is a more powerful force for managing my arthritis than the medication."

In Gabriella's battle with rheumatoid arthritis, a combination of possible triggers—genetics, stress, infections, chemical exposures—causes her immune system to designate her own joints as foreign and attack them. Under stress, her body can release hormones and chemicals that could worsen the problem, a "We're under attack, release the troops!" response. By engaging in the mental exercises associated with her joys, she calms her already aggravated immune system.

Gabriella's morning practice calls upon a bouquet of items from her Bliss List. And sometimes your Bliss List will point you to one great passion, so large and engrossing, that it alone generates great joy over a long period of time.

 What's your number one passion? Look for something that currently gives you much joy. You can also rank the items on your Bliss List. It's helpful to determine your top five and commit them to memory. That way, they're always there to help you.

POSTCARD FROM THE EDGE OF LIFE

The doctors in the intensive care unit of a busy urban medical center gave us insight into how Identification figures prominently in survival and eventual recovery. Among their non-comatose patients, they reported, those who feel emotionally defeated are less likely to recover. Assuming all other medical factors to be equal, people who stop caring about what they used to love are more likely to lose their will to live.

James, a twenty-year veteran physician of an intensive care unit, told us, "Those who make fast steps to recovery say, 'I have wonderful things to live for,' and are highly motivated by the thought of returning to their lives." James remembers some of his most successful patients: the airline pilot who vividly pictured himself back in the log cabin he painstakingly crafted with his own hands; the seamstress who imagined herself playing piano duets with her granddaughter again; the motorcycle accident victim who fought for his life so he could return to the mountain trails he cherished.

Research both on injured athletes and stroke victims indicates that using imagery after injury significantly speeds a return to full physical functioning. Your use of imagery isn't limited to imagining physical performance, however. It can also take you far beyond.

MONKS, PIANISTS, AND DIRTY OLD MEN

At eighty-nine, Jaime, a retired endocrinologist, imagines performance of a different sort. His roguish glory days from the 1940s, along with the women who accompanied him, remain very much alive in his brain. And he's more than happy to recount them at a moment's notice. It would be easy to label Jaime a dirty old man. But what is actually happening when he's remembering his sexual conquests in such detail?

"When I picture myself as the young man I was back then, I actually feel sexual, physically fit, and romantic."

Envisioning loving, sexual relationships and telling stories about them created a viable open space in Jaime's life for what has become an unexpected reality. Just before his eighty-ninth birthday, he met a charming "younger woman," who had some vivid memories, too: eight-four-year-old Petunia. They now share a loving relationship that's both emotional and physical, and they regale one another with some wildly florid stories!

Though it may seem strange to segue from a dirty old man to Tibetan monks, there is a startling correlation. When researchers studied the brains of monks as they engaged in compassionate meditation, the areas that lit up correlated to areas that light up when the body engages in physical activity. The scientists were surprised, but the monks weren't. The monks use meditation as preparation for compassionate action.

But you don't have to be a monk to benefit. In one amazing study, people who only thought about playing notes on a piano, versus another group that was really playing the notes for the same amount of time each day, ended up performing almost as well as those who had actually been playing on a keyboard. Envisioning, which is to say vibrant imagination, prepares us for optimal levels of performance—whether we're a monk, a pianist, or a dirty old man—and gives us the feelings of competence and capability necessary for Brilliant Health.

The Power of Envisioning

In each of the stories you just read, envisioning is used to generate positive emotions. It works so well because the brain, as the master planner for the body, begins preparing for virtually any physical state the mind creates. Before making an important presentation at a meeting, imagine yourself as a brilliant, confident, capable expert who will sweep in and knock the audience off its feet. Your imaginings can have the power to override any unconscious physical sabotage stemming from your anxiety and visions of poor performance. If you do this repeatedly, there's a good chance you'll be standing taller, with shoulders back, head high, and taking deep breaths. These may be the only positive changes of which you are consciously aware, but your body is simultaneously making thousands of mini adjustments as it literally becomes what your mind tells it to be.

Many studies have shown the extreme power of envisioning over immune response. Some of the results are astounding. In one study, a group of medical students were instructed to focus on increasing the number of certain circulating white blood cells through an imagery program. Lab measurements confirmed that they had indeed increased the cells. Remarkably, when they were asked to decrease the levels of those same white blood cells through imagery, the lab measurement showed fewer cells than their baseline scores. Imagery has provided excellent results in other clinical settings as well. One trained-imagery program resulted in half of its asthma participants decreasing or discontinuing their medications. Another improved mood and lowered pain in fibromyalgia, and still another reduced pain in sufferers of juvenile rheumatoid arthritis.

Envisioning also helps us with our medications. A recent series of studies on the placebo effect reported that, when patients are told about the expected impact of a pain medication like morphine, the painkilling effect could have almost double the impact than when the patients don't know what they're taking. The theory is that thinking about a drug's effectiveness and the belief that it will work generates biochemisty that combines with the drug's actual physical properties and amplifies its strength.

How We Do It: Imagery 101

To begin, define the outcome you would like to achieve. Is it improved symptoms during allergy season, better sleep, reduced anxiety, less low back pain, a strong body during cancer treatment, or a svelte, toned figure during an exercise and diet program?

Next, find an emotionally resonant and detailed image that you would enjoy visualizing several times a day. It should capture perfectly the best conceivable outcome, and it should be a picture that speaks to you. If you need help coming up with a specific, detailed image, turn to your Bliss List. As examples, picture walking up a mountain trail with greater endurance, breathing deeply and allergy-free in a beautiful garden, or stretching and dancing easily with gracefulness and without pain. If recovery from a disease is your outcome, use concrete images pertinent to your disease. An extreme example might be cancer. If you love *Star Trek*, you might choose to see yourself in a spaceship shooting down cancer cells and picture them exploding. If you love flowers, you might picture a beautiful garden where healthy cells bloom like roses, and cancer cells dry up and die.

Now that you have your image, there are many methods of imagery practice. You may want to capture the image on paper to remind you, or have music that is complementary to your vision. Some people have even recorded themselves or someone else reading a vision script to them. Other people use senses of smell, touch, or hearing to evoke a sense image.

Find ten to fifteen minutes when you won't be disturbed. Close your eyes. Start by bringing your attention inside your body to your breathing and your muscles. Ignore the critical, judgmental part of your brain that may tell you about all the stuff you should be doing. Spend time exploring your chosen image with as much sensory detail as you can conjure. Explore the world you have created. Enjoy it. It might become your reality.

The richer your image and the more fully you envision, the more you are conditioning your mind. You know how long it takes to train your body to learn something new, and it is the same for your mind. Initially, you may want to do this every day until those "mind muscles" are strong and agile and can envision on command. Eventually, the enjoyment and pleasure you get from the process will encourage you to flow into envisioning with little formal planning. And remember, the sensation of pleasure is a healthy state.

Using the guidelines in the preceding section, "How We Do It: Imagery 101," take yourself through a simple imagery exercise.

VOLENDAM

North of Amsterdam there's a small village called Volendam that sits on the edge of an enormous lake known as the Ijsselmeer. Volendam is one of many small towns that skirt the lake, and the people in these hamlets spend years anticipating a rare and much heralded event—when the lake freezes smooth. You might wonder why, beyond the opportunity to get in some ice skating, this is such an anticipated occurrence. When we were in Volendam several years ago we found out, for we had the amazing good fortune to be there on the very day (the first in several decades) that the Ijsselmeer actually froze over in one, smooth sheet.

As we watched the excited villagers don colorful winter wear and grab their ice skates, we realized that the frozen lake enabled all of the people living around it to transform the ice into a huge community as they skated and walked directly to villages that were usually much harder to get to. We soon understood the uniqueness of this event and our supreme luck at having stumbled upon it, and we were swept up in all of the magic. Each one of our five senses was firing as we took in the spectacle, and we snapped dozens of pictures so we could capture that memorable day.

After we returned home we eagerly awaited the day all the photographs from our trip were ready to be picked up from the photo shop. (This was before the advent of digital cameras.) We especially wanted to see our pictures from that wonderful, frozen experience on the Ijsselmeer. So try to imagine how we felt when, on picking up our photos, we learned that of all the rolls we'd brought in, one had been destroyed by the photo processing—the one with our pictures of Volendam.

We were heartbroken. "Why *that* roll?" we asked ourselves. In our minds, an irreplaceable life experience had disappeared.

But once we accepted the idea that the photographs were gone, we knew we had to somehow preserve our recollections while they were still vibrant.

We decided to commit to memory all of the sensations from that day: the growing excitement of the people as the news spread through the towns that the lake had frozen; the brilliant winter light and the colors of the big scarves, traditional costumes, and pointed bonnets the townspeople wore for their big day; the unmistakable swoosh of the gleaming skates as they cut across the smooth expanse of ice. What we wanted to capture most of all was the strange, wonderful sensation of walking out so far from the shoreline into the crisp cold of the northern European winter to share in the warmth and camaraderie of such a rare event.

Losing our photos forced us to reclaim that day in Volendam in a way we never would have otherwise. The small misfortune of those lost photos brought us something of greater value. It taught us how we can actually capture treasured memories, down to every glorious sight, sound, smell, and taste, more effectively than by relying on a simple paper photograph. Nowadays when we travel we don't just use pictures to remember things, we reimagine them, vividly, and it makes for much better storytelling once we return home.

After the next memorable event in your life, take a few moments to engage all of your senses. What did it feel like? What were the most vivid sights, sounds, textures, and tastes? This exercise will actually help you relive the event with the depth and richness of the way it felt when it was happening.

To complete the practice of Identification, we'll leave the internal process of envisioning and take you to the power of storytelling.

Telling the Stories of Your Life

Identification has extraordinary impact when we use our marvelous skill of conjuring and articulating stories. Think of stories as simply a sequence of internal images expressed externally as narrative. When we're telling a story about one of our peak experiences, we're having a joyful moment. By savoring the positive aspects of experiences, we are not only reexperiencing it but also creating stronger connections with others by allowing friends and family to relive it with us. In essence, we honor ourselves and our experiences by using the power of our voice. Retelling converts the memory of a past event into a present reality, where it becomes "my experience" and "my event" in this moment. This helps explain why older people love to tell favored stories repeatedly.

Rick remembers the pink flush in his grandma Emma's leathery cheeks every time she told what she considered to be the extremely "racy" story, circa 1915, of being "the only girl invited to play squash with the handsome young men" at the handball courts of Brighton Beach, New York. His other grandmother, Alice, roared with glee every time she reeled off the story of turn-of-the-century America and her large immigrant family's tone-deaf, accent-laden, and noisy rendition of "The Star-Spangled Banner" at their family circle meetings. If people hadn't been standing, no one would have known it was our national anthem.

Which of your stories gives you the greatest joy? Tell them to someone who will get enjoyment from them. How do you feel afterward? Were you momentarily transported to the actual event? Were you able to conjure any of the real physical sensations you might have felt when the story was actually happening?

ONCE UPON A TIME: STORIES AS HEALERS

Eve is a professional storyteller. We've watched her work magic, capturing imaginations in schools and in hospitals. With stories reflecting the breadth of human experience and emotion, she weaves tales that carry people on journeys of heroics and love, fear and forgiveness. Over time, Eve has seen her tales lift children with severe illness up the staircase of health and transport ailing adults to happier moods and faster healing.

Eve's belief that healing is facilitated by stories is well-substantiated by medical research. At the University of Maryland in Baltimore, researchers showed that laughter elicited by funny stories is linked to the healthy function of blood vessels, dilating the inner lining to improve blood flow. Humorous stories have been shown to reduce anxiety, stress, and tension, and to improve judgment, understanding, and perception. They also augment sociability and interpersonal interaction.

Beyond creating laughter, part of Eve's work is helping people tell their own stories, giving them importance and purpose. She talks about one of her hundreds of patients, a middle-aged man hospitalized with heart disease. As she entered his room, Eve saw a frail, bent over, crestfallen person. He shared the story of his illness, about being a patient, his doctors, his prognosis, his medications. Then Eve helped him shift the story away from disease. As he shared vignettes about his wife and grown children, his smart investments in California real estate, and his days as a navy pilot, his body began to straighten. His eyes brightened, his voice amplified, and his hands became animated. Nurses were astonished when they entered his room. Eve accompanied the man through a metamorphosis, from a story that was driven by sickness to a healthy story full of vitality. His body and mind reflected this experience. He told her, "No one talks to me. I need to talk about my real life. I haven't felt this well in a long time."

BE CAREFUL THE TALES YOU TELL; YOUR BODY WILL LISTEN

What are your favorite stories, sweet remembrances, funny recollections, proudest moments, and loving embraces? Tell yourself the story you want to hear about your body, your happiness, and your life. If they don't exist yet, invent them, in detail.

But also be careful *how* you tell them. Researchers at Northwestern University found strong correlations between people's levels of contentment and the way they tell stories about themselves. Those with "mood problems" might have vivid memories, but they're often tainted by dark details. "The graduation was beautiful, but someone said something unkind to me." "The trip was enjoyable, but it rained one entire day."

By contrast, those likely to be the most energetic and civic-minded tend to tell stories in the reverse. A disappointing event typically leads to something positive. "I broke my leg skiing but met lots of wonderful people in the lodge." "I had the flu last week, but I got to read a new novel." "The earthquake gave me a chance to bond with my neighbors."

The two of us have found that it's important to evaluate the stories we tell others because they have such powerful impact on how positively or negatively we feel about our lives. Ask yourself these questions: Are your stories "victimy," hostile, or critical tales that end in negativity? Or are they optimistic, positive, forward-looking, and funny stories?

Tell a story about a negative event or period in your life. Now tell it with a positive spin. Add nurturing emotions, warmth, and affirmative interpretations. The more you retell the story with its positive elements, the more contentment and sense of control you'll have over that part of your life. Be sure to share it with someone.

A decade ago, we interviewed an extraordinary elderly woman in Amsterdam whose family had been killed by the Nazis in World War Two. Amazingly, her story included not just the war years but consistently noted the fact that her family had lived happily and affluently as Dutch Jews for four hundred years. In her story, the traumatic years were dramatic and important, but merely one terrible and frightening five-yearlong anomaly in an otherwise remarkable and vibrant history. Through most of the tale of her life, she beamed at us.

During traumatic events like a death of a loved one, a car accident, sudden loss of a relationship, health issues, or a job change, our brains may become flooded with stress hormones and messengers. These dangerously high levels of glucocorticoids can block and even damage the area in the brain responsible for intellectually processing memories.

Stories allow us to process stressful experiences and memories in a way that reduces the harmful effects of stress. Instead of continually being the person experiencing the event, we simply become the teller of the story, shifting our brain from painful experiencing to higher brain functions of rationality and creativity. This is the same beneficial effect some forms of meditation teach us in "becoming the observer to our distress."

The shift from emotional reaction to dispassionate storyteller is well-illustrated in research. In a brain activation study, when people were asked to become emotionally *involved and empathize* with a photo of someone in pain, all lower regions are activated. But when asked to *tell* a story about the person in pain, higher brain areas were activated, shifting from emotionally disturbed to intellectually processing brain functions.

The organization Compassionate Friends is dedicated to helping families deal with the death of a child. It offers a safe place for people to talk about the lives and deaths of their children and their parental grief, something society at large doesn't want to hear about. When we had the opportunity to speak with a chapter chairwoman, she told us, "I know firsthand how storytelling helps diminish grief. Telling it over and over lessens the emotional charge, because it becomes your story as you tell it, rather than the raw experience of your child dying. Although the sadness never goes away, the pain becomes more bearable."

KAITLYN'S STORY: TACTILE ENVISIONING

All of our five senses can be powerful, health-inducing elements of our stories. Kaitlyn gives us an inspiring look into why.

Once upon a time Kaitlyn was an eighteen-year-old who had never had a menstrual period. After a great deal of evaluation, the doctor told Kaitlyn that she would never have children. "My entire identity was wrapped around someday being a mother. I felt devastated and wronged. How could I be myself if I couldn't have children of my own?"

Seven years pass. Kaitlyn has still not had a menstrual cycle and has again been told she would never have children. As she walks down a street, she's reminded by a toy store window display that she must buy a birthday present for a friend's young daughter. Kaitlyn picks up a life-size baby doll and it feels extremely good. Holding it feels so good, in fact, that she's overwhelmed by an extraordinary maternal urge, overcomes her embarrassment at the "weirdness" of the sensation, and buys the doll for herself. Kaitlyn loves the doll, holds it whenever she can, carries it with her, and indulges in the sensations and delights of what she described to us as "conjured motherhood."

Three months later, at age twenty-five, Kaitlyn had her first period. As of this writing, her cycle has been absolutely regular for five years. Whether she has children or not is yet to be seen. But her tactile form of envisioning may well have had powerful effects on her body's hormonal production.

Identification

This is only one woman's story. In no way does it suggest that physically conjuring motherhood will guarantee fertility. It does, however, illustrate that storytelling comes in many powerful forms and can include all our senses. Among these many styles are the verbalized stories we tell to others, our internal dialogue, and Kaitlyn's tale of tactile envisioning.

All the people who told us their stories have used the practice of Identification in their own unique ways to convert fears, anxieties, and hostilities into a state of well-being. In years to come, we may understand fully the biochemical changes created by envisioning and exactly how these changes benefit us at the cellular level. Until then, we know that imagery, envisioning, and storytelling have brightened human life from its beginnings, and we can all cultivate its powers on our own behalf.

We started this chapter by naming our passions (the Bliss List), moved to the power of envisioning them, and then showed how we can breathe life into these visions through words by telling stories about them. Now it's time to complete the continuum by taking action.

Only passions, great passions, can elevate the soul to great things.

—DENIS DIDEROT (1713–1784)

FOUR

Centrality

*One thing life has taught me: if you are interested, you
never have to look for new interests. They come to you.
When you are genuinely interested in one thing, it will
always lead to something else.*

—ELEANOR ROOSEVELT (1884–1962)

After more than a decade of studying happiness and health,
there's something we can say with complete confidence: It's
impossible to attain Brilliant Health without *doing* the things
you love. How can you be fully, completely healthy if you're
not infused with the positive emotions that come from doing
things that exhilarate you?

*The fourth practice is Centrality: making central to your life the
things you love by acting on them.* When life gets busy or you face
illness, it's easy to lose sight of your passions, but this is when
you need them the most. Living your Centralities may take
creativity, unbridled imagination, and single-minded assertion.
But by insisting on it, you move yourself up the Brilliant
Health staircase to a feeling of true fulfillment. Once initiated,
it's a self-perpetuating cycle: engaging in your Centralities
makes you more Brilliantly Healthy, and being in Brilliant

Health gives you the energy to keep engaging in your Centralities.

Our advice is simple: just do it! If you're rejuvenated each time you go camping, then you can't afford to let your tent gather dust in the garage. If you love contemporary art, it's a given that you'll attend the sculpture exhibit you've wanted to see. If hosting a backyard barbecue with friends makes you feel fully alive, your grill is sure to be fired up all summer long.

Living Your Centralities: How and Why

If Brilliant Health Identification (chapter 3) is uncovering, envisioning, and telling stories about our greatest passions, Centrality is all about action. Here, once again, your Bliss List is indispensable. When we centralize, we ask ourselves, "What's at least one item from my Bliss List I can *do* today?" For more elaborate passions we ask, "What's at least one step I can take toward realizing this passion?" And when it comes to Centralities, variety is the spice of life. Researchers have shown that greater happiness is directly related to an increase in the number and diversity of pleasurable events we engage in daily.

Intuitively, it makes sense that the things that uplift and stimulate us emotionally do the same for our bodies. An impressive longitudinal study of 20,000 adults showed that doing what we love increases our satisfaction levels, which correlates strongly with greater longevity. Just prior to his hundredth birthday, the comedian George Burns was asked the secret to his long life. He replied, "I've spent almost a century doing what I love best."

From Montevideo to Monte Carlo, the variety, breadth, and uniqueness of Centrality stories we've heard over the years never ceases to amaze us. And we've loved hearing every one of them. Here's one thing we've learned: it's of critical importance for each one of us to pursue the things we love without fear or embarrassment, no matter how unconventional they may be or what others may think of them.

Since the two of us are always searching for our next health-and-happiness interview, we make it a habit to keep our eyes and ears open for them. And finding a good one is way up there on our Bliss List. We often stumble upon them in the most unlikely or unexpected places. While riding the Long Island Railroad recently, we met a guy who introduced himself as Josh the Lobsterman. Exuberant and thoughtful, he looked younger than his forty-something years and attributed good health and youthfulness, surprisingly, to his work. He wakes up each day at four a.m. bristling with excitement about the day ahead. For Josh, chilly mornings, hauling heavy, cumbersome, lobster-laden traps is a kind of heaven. He also has a love of Eastern philosophy. "You know what Confucius says," Josh declared. "Find a job you love, and you never work a day in your life."

We met twenty-five-year-old Roland at an antebellum mansion in Louisiana. He told us he'd go almost anywhere in the country to have a chance to see memorabilia about the Civil War. Helene, an accountant we met in a Parisian café, told us how she looks forward to each Saturday when she devotes herself to creating miniature Polaroid photo transfers on scraps of wood. In a flush of enthusiasm, she took us to her home to show us her artwork.

Notice how you feel when you're doing what you love. And notice how you feel when you're doing something about which you're *not* passionate. If you're not doing the things that bring you joy, get out your Bliss List. Each day of the next week, pick at least one item, and make sure to do it.

But of all the Centrality stories we've heard, one of the most classic examples comes from our favorite nun.

SISTER MARY GLADYS AND THE DAMMIT DOLLS

On an arid bluff overlooking an expanse of rolling Canadian prairie sits a convent. It once housed 1,500 Franciscan sisters and is now inhabited by 150 elderly women who run the facility as a conference center. In winter, the exterior reminds us of a Gothic mansion: bleak, frozen terrain with patches of snow and a foreboding architecture. The paucity of the landscape and harshness of the buildings suggest cold, unhappy people living inside. It's easy to speculate that they have nothing. And, in a material sense, it's true.

As expected, inside the heavy oak doors are drafty stone hallways and cold, imposing arches. Tucked into a dark alcove, however, blooms a bright, colorful little gift store. Hundreds of sewn dolls, teddy bears, colorful blankets and pillows, mittens and jackets are bursting off shelves and overflowing their baskets. Especially fascinating are the dammit dolls piled high in the boutique. They're overstuffed and multicolored with long legs and instructions attached. The owner is advised to grasp each leg and repeatedly bash the doll to relieve stress all the while yelling, "Dammit, dammit, dammit!"

The whole idea delighted us, and on our first trip we bought a few dozen to give as gifts. Learning that the dammit dolls are the brainchild of ninety-two-year-old Sister Mary Gladys was even more intriguing.

On our second trip we were greeted by Sister Mary Gladys herself, who apparently wanted to meet "the two handsome young men from California." (For that comment alone we immediately loved her.) Tall, slender, and smiling, she greeted us at the door and told us how pleased she was that her art was making it all the way to the West Coast. At ninety-two, her health is excellent. We asked her secret. With complete directness she said, "Sewing. It is my greatest passion. When I'm sewing, all worries disappear, and I have a wonderful sense of calm. Without it I would wither and die. I can't wait to get up each morning and start to sew. Now, mind you," she twinkled, "I don't stuff the dammit dolls. Sister Lolita loves to do that. And she's ninety-eight!"

How often do Sisters Mary Gladys and Lolita smack the dammit dolls? Their reply: "We don't need to!"

Sister Mary Gladys was not only fit as a fiddle, she was sharp as a tack. It's no wonder. If we're doing what we love, we don't just feel better, we keep our brains sharp. In several studies looking at memory, people perform much better when what they're doing is charged with emotional relevance. By doing things that bring you joy, you are feeding your brain for better performance by actively engaging multiple neuronal pathways.

But we can't all be like Sister Mary Gladys. It's clear that most of us mere mortals have bills to pay, family responsibilities, and can't spend all of our time living our Centralities. But even in situations where there doesn't seem to be enough time, money, or control over life, we need to be careful not to fall into the self-deception of living for the future instead of now. Happiness and quality of life are hung up like swimsuits in the dead of winter every time we say, "I'll have time for passions when I am . . ." graduated, or retired, or an executive, or married, or single, or whatever.

We've done our own research during some of our corporate workshops. We've asked more than four hundred people from all walks of life one simple question: "When you feel emotionally down, what do you do to elevate your mood?" ninety-two percent of the responses fall into the Centrality category, like listening to favorite music, engaging in a favorite sport, and spending time with loved ones.

So it appears that most of us already know the curative power of doing what we love. It's just that we don't find ways to do it more often. We should or we may consign ourselves to a life of smashing dammit dolls. And centralities not only benefit our health, they also play into our success.

Centrality: A Key to Success

We have had the pleasure of working with medical students and university graduate students in accelerated degree programs with high-pressure, aggressive curriculums. The students are overloaded with fourteen-hour days of class and homework.

Although we may think a single-minded, nose-to-the-grindstone approach would lead to the most success, the students who thrive physically, emotionally, and academically are *not* those who study the hardest. Rather, the most successful people insist on taking small blocks of time each day to indulge in doing something they enjoy. In our classes, we encourage them to take the time for simple pleasureable activities like bike riding with a spouse, fixing a pot of spaghetti for friends, or catching a new documentary film.

For our students, taking control over just a small amount of time each day prevents the out-of-control feeling in an entirely overly scheduled day and diminishes the impact of stress, thus allowing them to be more focused, efficient, and effective at their work. And even more exciting, studies in both rats and people show that perceived control over currently stressful events is actually protective against the biological impact of stress about uncontrollable future events. When we master stress in the present by engaging our Centralities every day, we can further lower stress levels by trusting our emotional capability to deal with it in the future.

How much time a day are you engaged in activities you love? How much of this can you change right now? Spend a few moments with your Bliss List and your schedule. Decide how much time you can devote to your passions. Maybe it's five hours a week to start. More? Less? Consider enlisting a family member, spouse, or friend to help you schedule time for passions, for play, and for fun. Think big, like planning a trip to Italy in a year, and small, like picking up a book of Italian for fifteen minutes every day.

Be creative, take a risk, and throw embarrassment out the window. Keep a diary, and set an intention to be accountable to your passions, just as you are to your career, family, and values.

Our students graduate eventually. But wrestling with Centrality is never done. Because jobs are such a big part of life let's take a look at the connection between our jobs and our Centralities.

De-"Centralized" Corporate Life

As we consult with leaders from large corporations, we often see people who neither effectively manage their health nor live their passions. By conforming to demanding corporate cultures, they may avoid rocking the boat, but they end up with gut-wrenching internal conflicts because they're not doing what they truly enjoy and quickly fall out of integrity with themselves.

Grab another chance to use your higher brain. Regardless of your job, find ways to enjoy it by using the best of your strengths and passions. In most workplace settings, as long as you are embracing the company's values and turning out a high-quality product, you have the creative opportunity to be intentional about how you approach the job. Challenge yourself to build in your Centralities.

Sometimes, integrating our passions with our work is impossible. What do we do? Meet Jack.

HIT THE ROAD, JACK

Two things were guaranteed to stop baby Jack from crying: music and TV. As Jack grew, he would bounce to music on the radio while he watched movies. By the time he was a teenager, he had become a full-fledged film aficionado, amateur jazz pianist, and well-paid professional disc jockey.

After graduating from college with dual degrees in film composition and music business, he was the top pick out of four hundred applicants for a much-coveted job with a global entertainment conglomerate. At twenty-two, he landed in a chic office on the thirty-eighth floor of a Times Square highrise with an enviable salary and generous benefits. By all normal professional standards, he had arrived. But soon, Jack wasn't feeling his usual upbeat self. In fact, within a few months, he was absolutely miserable.

"To everyone else, I was amazingly successful. But being stuck in a hermetically sealed building working on monotonous copyright issues didn't turn out to be my idea of success. It couldn't have been any more remote from my musical interests. I was working long hours and felt I'd lost control over my life."

Meanwhile, Jack began to feel terrible pain in his hands and back, which grew to nearly paralyzing proportions. After multiple trips to specialists in New York City, Jack got the diagnosis: psoriatic arthritis, a serious autoimmune illness that destroys bones and joints.

"Psoriatic arthritis (PA) was a perfect match with the company. I didn't feel my life was my own, and with PA in full swing, neither was my body. Work was miserable, my body was miserable. I finally got so disabled that I couldn't type or play tennis or piano. Even though I avoided dealing with my issues about work, my body forced me to deal with the PA. As I did, the disease also made me confront why I wasn't happy."

Jack saw that he'd miscast himself: right industry, wrong job. Since his Centralities weren't part of his professional life, he was perpetually under stress and in a state of crisis. We know that sustained high levels of stress deregulate our immune systems. Jack's was looking for an enemy, any enemy, to attack and, combined with his genetic predisposition and past history, his miserable work situation triggered his PA. Fundamentally, Jack attacked himself.

Jack may have become somewhat numb to the regular stress of going in to work every day, yet his body was sending him increasingly louder messages all along the way. If we don't listen to our body when it gives us a gentle buzzer alarm, it sometimes ramps up with a fire engine siren, then a screeching tornado warning. These alarms are critical indicators of when we are *not* centralizing our passions.

While still working at his "decentralized job," Jack's doctors prescribed a miracle drug to suppress the painful symptoms of PA, but its side effects made him prone to serious respiratory illness. In his first four months on medication, he took five separate courses of antibiotics to kill off opportunistic infections. On one occasion, an emergency trip to the hospital for pneumonia landed him in intensive care.

Jack finally left work on disability, giving him a chance to revisit his love of music and movies. He knew in his heart returning to corporate life would disable him permanently. Jack began to explore alternatives, visiting with friends and meeting with industry sources. Fourteen months later, he began the first of a series of jobs making independent films, and he found the work thrilling. On his first job, the PA-related symptoms lessened significantly.

Two years later, without a single dose of antibiotics, Jack has vastly reduced his dependence on immunosuppressive medications. Meanwhile, his deep interest in film has rocketed him into a producer's position. "I'm told the psoriatic arthritis will be with me for life, but the pain is gone, and I'm not sick. I don't define myself by my illness anymore but by the work I love. And the work makes me feel great."

We do need to be careful in this discussion. Not all stress is unhealthy. Some kinds of acute, short-term stress, the natural outcome of a fulfilling life, have positive effects on our immune function. After all, a wedding is stressful, and so is a new baby, a new relationship, or a new business. It's chronic or frequent stress that's destructive. Though your body may adjust to a chronic stressor over time, it remains erosive and can hypersensitize you to any type of stress.

 What items from your Bliss List are impossible to do at work? How could you more actively build them into your home life?

Passions and Demons

Just as Jack used Centrality as a potent medicine, Tony was able to replace his demons. Over a traditional German dinner,

Tony, now twenty-seven, took us through his history. As early as age two, he demanded his parents perform certain intricate daily rituals, and throughout childhood he exhibited anxieties about his body and surrounding environment that persisted into his teen years. In high school, Tony also became increasingly angry, not at the usual adolescent frustrations but at what he perceived to be an unjust world full of discrimination and prejudice. Rallying around every underdog at school and lashing out at adult authority figures, he wasn't afraid to go up against anyone or anything in the name of justice. He may have been popular with his peers but he certainly wasn't with school officials. His defiance got him expelled twice.

At sixteen, Tony was diagnosed with a severe form of obsessive-compulsive disorder (OCD), a mysterious neurological syndrome involving receptors in various parts of the brain, and in which recurring unwanted thoughts (obsessions) are difficult to stop and repetitive actions (compulsions) are carried out in an attempt to relieve those thoughts. Even at its best, Tony's OCD interfered with his ability to go about daily activities. At its worst, it confined him at home where fears of the outside world enveloped him. Concerns about food contamination, stepping on dirty needles, and superstitious beliefs that dire things would happen to him and his family if he didn't complete certain elaborate tasks became almost too much to bear.

Five years of therapy, experimental treatments, medical specialists, and a host of drug interventions produced only small improvements. Although doctors advised that he'd "just have to learn to live with it," Tony refused to accept that prognosis, deciding instead to take matters into his own hands. "I didn't want fifty percent of a life. I wanted to feel hundred percent joy, which meant finding solutions so that it wouldn't exist at all."

But something fascinating happened. The very thing that kept getting him in trouble might now be his salvation. Tony saw the more he obsessed, the worse things got. He also noticed that when he was immersed in moral indignation at an unjust world, his symptoms vastly diminished. Using the brain's ability to focus fully on only one thing at a time, he forced himself to think about external injustices rather than inner compulsions. "My answer was to redirect my rage into passion, which then became my greatest motivator. I turned myself into an activist for social change. Here was my remedy for OCD."

Tony's intention was to fully harness the power of his newly articulated passion. He was fascinated by Martin Luther King Jr., Allen Ginsburg, and the antiwar movement of the '60s. Searching for his own way to express his ideals, Tony gravitated toward helping children. Working his way up to lead teacher at a children's center, he became responsible for thirty-five preschoolers in the mornings, and elementary-aged kids in an after-school program, all from impoverished minority families without English-language skills. He was outraged that many had no food on the table at home, were neglected in various ways, and lacked the necessities granted to other American children.

While most of the other teachers were satisfied letting the kids play in the schoolyard, Tony dedicated his evenings to crafting lesson plans that taught the kids about respect, about refusing to see themselves as victims, and about how to find opportunities and act on them. He set up tutoring programs for homework and customized reading techniques. "The commitment to these kids required every ounce of brainpower I had to give, and I was so into it that I didn't have a chance to obsess."

As Tony's story makes clear, values-driven Centralities bring positive results. The students' parents credit Tony with saving their children and, miraculously, his OCD symptoms are non-existent when he's on the job. After work, his symptoms usually return, but he's learning how to divert ever more of his attention to his passions.

Centrality in Balance

For us, the realm of Centrality and its effects came into clearer focus in a place known for its extreme contrasts and crystal-clear light: Africa. While training AIDS doctors at the University of Cape Town, we interviewed Dr. Nigel, an expert and champion in his field. Treating thousands with this cruel disease, he understands that long-term survival for AIDS patients in South Africa is currently unlikely. But for those who live longest and best, he says, "It's all how they place their illness. It must be a priority, but it mustn't be the only priority. My best patients aggressively manage their illness but also aggressively do the things they love to do. It's a balancing act, really."

The notion of balancing health management and personal passions is of great importance when working with serious illness. But, as it turns out, Dr. Nigel's insight has been extremely helpful in our work with patients, leaders of global corporations, and our students in high-pressure postgraduate programs.

With Tony's OCD, overriding his symptoms with Centrality is an extremely positive and creative response to a problem. But it isn't a cure-all. We need a balance. And sometimes, at the other end of the spectrum, Centralities mask important physical signals our bodies are transmitting.

When William Shakespeare used the phrase "too much of a good thing" in *As You Like It*, he couldn't have issued a better warning about Centralities. When we are overly engaged with our passions, much of our attention is diverted, and we're more than able to ignore messages from our body. Often this works in our favor. But think of any time you have pushed too far physically, disregarded messages from your body, and suffered injury. Perhaps you've stayed up late working on a completely engaging project, only to get sick. Or you're completely in the flow of a sport, but afterward, you feel the pain of overexertion. You've had too much of a good thing.

What If You Can't Live Your Centrality Anymore?

Realistically, many of us are far less likely to be engulfed by our passions than we are to be forced to delay or actually replace our Centralities because of life circumstances. It would be unrealistic for any of us to assume that we will be able to live the same passions for a lifetime. What happens when we can't?

HITTING THE WALL AND CASTING OVER IT

Terry loved everything about fly fishing: the thrill of rainbow trout gulping flies on the water's surface, the serenity of the forest, and best of all, planting herself dead center in the rushing waters of her beloved Idaho rivers. But when Terry learned she had leukemia and was facing months of aggressive chemotherapy and isolation from others to create a more sterile environment, she took a steep dive into the panic zone.

"My first response was shock. Then came outright fear and hostility. I knew they were natural responses, but I also knew they wouldn't help me."

Coincidentally, Terry had recently attended one of our seminars and had been particularly taken by the notion of assertively living Centralities and thought they might help her now. In Terry's case, however, fly-fishing was an impossible match with chemotherapy and isolation.

But Terry got creative. Before her first treatment, she purchased a fly-tying kit and hired an expert to teach her the art of making her own flies. She also ordered two dozen books and catalogs on fishing, rods, and reels. "Once treatment began, I tied flies whenever I felt up to it and immersed myself in the books, studying techniques for the barrel roll cast and for how to land a five-pound brookie. On days when I couldn't raise my head from the pillow, I simply looked forward to the next time I could get my hands on those books."

For the eight-week treatment period, whenever Terry felt fear, loneliness, and hostility begin to take over, she dove straight into her bedside version of Centrality. At a time when many would feel depressed and wallow in self-pity, Terry refused to tumble down the Brilliant Health staircase. Instead, she maximized the small portion of her life she could control. She ended up with dual Centralities: the bedside version and the active one. These days, she can often be found standing in the fast-moving waters of Idaho, casting flies of her own making.

Terry's story dovetails with a large body of research on emotions. Chronic hostility, cynicism and bitterness are related not only to having fewer friends but to significant health risks. In a study of more than six hundred women, high levels of hostility were associated with more severe coronary artery disease and worse chest pain. In another study they correlated with increased insulin resistance (one factor in the development of diabetes) and elevated glucose levels. If we replace our negative reactions with joy that comes from living our centralities, we stand ourselves in good stead.

If you're currently dealing with an illness that gets in the way of your Centralities, can you figure out new ways to integrate them back into your life? Or are there other passions or interests that might work better?

Terry's story highlights the beauty of finding innovative ways to count on our existing Centralities like old friends. But what about when it's impossible to pursue our greatest loves?

HITTING THE WALL AND DOING AN ABOUT-FACE

As a former biochemistry college student and gymnast, Jen, our medical collaborator, took pride in attaining high levels of physical and mental activity: doing ten-mile hikes before class, rock climbing, and excelling in quantum mechanics courses. For Jen, strenuous physical activities and competitive intellectual challenges were her great sources of joy. Until, she hit the wall.

"The first wall was quite literal. I was in a car accident, and my car flew into a wall." Though her injuries forced her to stop most physical activity, and she struggled to excel in intensive schoolwork, she tried to maintain her same old Centralities.

The second wall was another kind of wall entirely. In the first year of medical training she was diagnosed with type I diabetes. Before this happened, small messages from her body about pain, fatigue, and weakness were physical challenges to be overcome. Now, ignoring any of these messages could precipitate a rapid decline into hypoglycemia, a dangerous condition. And the unpredictable eating and exercise schedules that were a part of her medical school life made her glucose levels fluctuate, which also made rigorous intellectual competition difficult.

With intellect and body failing, she had the forced opportunity to self-analyze. "I realized that my former Centralities could no longer be sources of joy and motivation. And, in fact, they were based on performance and competition and allowed very little expression of the true me. It was time for a change in priorities. I needed to go back, reevaluate, and find a new spark of passion and drive."

As she evaluated her life, she also found herself questioning what she felt were shortcomings in the traditional medical model. Reducing illness into "cellular compartments" meant missing the holism of the person with the disease. She believed the divisions between the realms of the mind and body were artificial and questioned the reliance on drugs and surgery coupled with the lack of preventative care. The lack of self-care for patients and for physicians also concerned her. Removed from a competitive, performance frame of mind, she found herself becoming a spokesperson for the reintegration of mind and body.

Motivated by hitting the wall of diabetes, Jen created a new life for herself. She says, "New Centralities led into my unexpected and innovative new career path: doing research into mind-body connections, bringing rigorous science to the world of wellness, and getting to be on the forefront of how medicine is changing."

Jen's search for new Centralities also highlights an ability to find new meaning in illness, trauma, and injury, which are all hallmarks of our next tool in the Brilliant Health model: Recasting.

The more passions and desires one has, the more ways one has of being happy.

—CATHERINE-CHARLOTTE DE GRAMONT (1639–1678),

Princess of Monaco and Mistress of Louis XIV

FIVE

Recasting

A wise man should consider that health is the greatest of
human blessings, and learn how by his own thought to
derive benefit from his illnesses.

—HIPPOCRATES (460 BC–377 BC), *Regimen in Health*

Fear, anger, grief, and despair: each is an inevitable part of our
life and important to embrace. Yet each has the potential to
seriously hurt our body if allowed to persist. Being in a perpetual state of *anger* worsens many cardiovascular conditions
and increases carotid artery stiffness. A deep and chronic *despair* is depression, a stress state associated with increased sus-
ceptibility to infection, worsening symptoms and exacerbations
in many diseases, and a risk factor in developing Alzheimer's
disease. *Fear*, particularly panic, puts increased stress on the
heart, increases respiration, and shuts down digestion.

We can't always stay in positive emotions. No matter how
good our lives are, all of us will face grief and emotional
pain. Loved ones will die, careers will falter, and we'll all confront illness. The question is, what do we do with the stress
and pain that results? How do we cope with the worst life

throws at us while continuing our climb on the staircase of Brilliant Health?

The answer is found in the fifth practice, Recasting, the process for moving through trauma and illness by converting negative emotions into meaning, opportunity, and action.

Recasting empowers you to feel the full force of your emotions and ultimately use them to your benefit. Identified a dozen years ago during our early happiness research, Recasting is the name we gave to a remarkable yet practical process used universally by the extremely happy people we met. From architects in Atlanta to farmers in the French countryside, we saw Recasting applied consistently to life's most stressful events. Even though most of these people had never read a self-help book or taken a personal growth seminar, somehow they intuitively adopted the process and relied on it. As you'll soon see, the chronic nonhealers take a very different path.

Since those early days we've adapted Recasting to move individuals, families, and even communities through pain and suffering into happier and healthier lives. It's a process that's perfectly designed for returning to the positive emotions we need to be in Brilliant Health. We've been particularly inspired and moved by the creativity people have used in Recasting their health problems and want to share some of their stories with you.

Getting Ready to Recast

It's important to clarify something up front: Recasting is very different from the commonly used term, *reframing*. In reframing, negative perceptions are quickly flip-flopped to the positive. Although reframing can be helpful for small problems, it's not the answer for significant life events. Ask any doctor or nurse working with the seriously ill, and they'll tell you how overly positive comments to patients often come out as trite sayings or folklore that cause unintended damage and hurt: "Someday you'll see the silver lining in all this." "God only gives you what you can handle." "Everything happens for a reason." But the "silver lining," the "reason," or "God's challenges" can be irrelevant, infuriating, or hurtful to someone who is suffering from grief or trauma.

Recasting is not about Pollyanna thinking or making lemonade out of lemons. There are some events that will always be lemons: sad, fear-inducing, or maddening. With Recasting we learn to deal with them as a natural part of life, extract their value, and then, when we are able, return to a happy life. We don't allow them to pervade our entire existence or become our identity. The exact opposite of denial, Recasting accepts the reality of any trauma or illness and constructs a context around it, leaving us in a more emotionally capable, elevated, and powerful state of mind.

Recasting has three phases:

• Feel your feelings.

• Find meaning.

• Recognize opportunities.

Phase One: Feel Your Feelings

When you deal with the big stuff—a traumatic or highly stressful event—there's nowhere else to start but with your emotions. Skipping the feelings phase of Recasting is like attempting to build the walls of a house before laying the foundation.

When it comes to Brilliant Health, and Recasting specifically, emotions are our best guides. They're not touchy-feely, nebulous, intangible states of being. And they aren't self-indulgent. Rather, they're brilliantly hardwired biochemical reactions that both motivate us to act and give us feedback about what's already happened. Think of them as *e-motions*. They're there to *move* us to a better place.

E-motions are a primal survival mechanism, an efficient and perfectly designed shortcut allowing us to bypass lengthy analysis. It would take far too long to intellectually process all the sensations we receive in any one moment. In fact, it would be ridiculous. For survival, a caveman out on a hunt needed to make instantaneous decisions and move quickly. If a dangerous wild boar was in the bushes, the caveman didn't have the luxury to analyze, "Okay, my vision sees leaves rustling; I hear a muffled grunt; and boy, that sure is a putrid smell! I wonder if all of these sensations mean something?" If he went through this lengthy process, he'd be gored, or his intended dinner would be long gone. Instead, in a millisecond, his brain translates and packages every sensory input into the emotions of excitement about potential food or fear of a potential predator. His e-motions have efficiently prepared his body for hair-trigger action.

But there's another class of e-motion that instructs us to take protective *inaction*. Fast-forward 10,000 years. You, the caveman's descendant, can probably identify with the tired, depressed feeling you have while lying in bed with a cold or flu. That lack of energy isn't due to the virus. It's your body's way to slow you down using messengers (called cytokines) that cause action-negative e-motions, so it can rally all its resources to fight the infection.

As we use them in Recasting, e-motions are our guide to what's important in life and offer a kind of instantaneous wisdom that works beautifully in partnership with our intellect. They quickly motivate, protect, and educate us, yet are also highly responsive to the way we think and how we behave. And dealing with our emotions is key to managing illness.

THE VALUE OF EXPRESSING YOUR FEELINGS

In 1989, what is now considered landmark medical research noted the physical benefits of expressing all varieties of emotions. Women with metastatic breast cancer were divided into two groups, one that participated in weekly support groups, the other getting only standard cancer therapy. "The sessions became a time and a place for women to express some of their deepest fears," explained head researcher Dr. Spiegel. One participant referred to her fear as "that sense of waking up at three in the morning with an elephant sitting on your chest." She added, "I wonder if I will live to see my son graduate from high school or my daughter get married. I have to keep up a front everywhere else—that's so hard." Spiegel also reported a "good deal of crying in these groups, as well as laughter . . . the groups provided a setting in which they could deal with their fears."

While long-term survival rates have soared for metasticized breast cancer in the years since this study was conducted, the findings of Dr. Spiegel's work are profound to this day. The group members, who actively shared feelings, lived twice as long on average as the control subjects (36.6 months for the group members versus an average of 18.9 months for the others). And the group members reported experiencing 50 percent less pain.

We want to emphasize that this approach isn't about positive thinking. Its benefit comes from the open expression of *all* emotions, a hallmark of this phase of Recasting.

THE MARRIAGE OF YOUR EMOTIONAL AND RATIONAL BRAIN: HOW TO UNCOVER TRUE EMOTIONS

To begin the Recasting process, you'll need to describe to yourself clearly the nature of the problem or issue with which you are dealing. Whether it's a stressful situation at work, a death, a relationship problem, or an illness, you should craft a careful portrait in your mind.

With that clear picture, you're in an ideal position to dig deep until you uncover one or more of the primary emotions you're experiencing as a result of the problem. The primary emotions are *sadness*, *anger*, *fear*, and *joy*. They're clear, unencumbered signposts of what you're truly feeling. If you identify feelings like anxiousness, surprise, jealousy, or worry, try again. These secondary emotions are either a "lite" version of a primary emotion or a blurry synthesis of two or more of them, which will divert you from the straightforward path of healing. If at all possible, go for the underlying, clear-cut, root feeling. For instance, after a troubling health diagnosis the anxiety you feel may be a combination of underlying fear and anger. Or it could be masking sadness. The primary emotion will set the direction you take in the following two phases of Recasting.

If you need help, try talking with another person. Verbalizing an emotion validates and confirms what you're feeling. As you verbalize, you may also realize that the emotion sounds off target, which gives you a chance to look deeper. Journaling is another powerful technique because the process of writing things down exposes your emotions to the scrutiny of your rational mind.

And what about people who suppress their emotions? Sometimes we're afraid of our feelings or simply not willing to deal with them. Being in a state of denial may help us survive trauma in the very short term, but in the long run it prevents our healing. In this first phase of Recasting, we need to figure out our real e-motions and let them guide the process.

Phase Two: Finding Meaning

Next, we enrich the Recasting process by bringing in our intellect to provide the analysis of what the problem or trauma means and what it can teach us. Here are five questions to consider in the second phase:

- What can I learn from all of this?

- What was my part in creating this?

- What does this issue say about me or about the way I've been behaving?

- What do I believe is the genesis of the problem?

- What are my feelings telling me?

There's a lot of gold to mine here. Illness, in particular, can be one of our greatest teachers. Though the following examples are not specific to any particular problem, you may come up with answers that sound like these: "My family is overwhelming me." "I'm learning life is far more fragile than I previously thought." "I'm making my symptoms worse by dwelling on them." "I haven't been eating well or exercising." "I need to be more honest with others." "I have to deal with things head-on." "I need to spend more quality time with my children." "I'm relying too much on family genetics rather than making healthy choices."

Most of us would agree that our greatest times of learning and growth have happened during times of hardship and pain rather than when life is rolling along smoothly. By sticking with this search for meaning, we open up a world of valuable material that leads to new information, insight, and profound understanding of ourselves. Not only do we learn about ourselves, we also receive physical benefits because learning and analysis keep our higher brain functions at full throttle.

Phase Three: Recognizing Opportunity

Phase Three involves a simple question with an abundance of answers. The question is: "Given my emotions (Phase One) and the meaning I've discovered around this problem (Phase Two), what new *opportunities* exist for me?

This phase embodies reimagining at its best. Just like in Identification, where telling stories lifts us up mentally and reduces stress, the final phase of Recasting infuses our life with the opportunities that allow us to move forward and away from the debilitation and hurt of a terrible life experience.

Finding new opportunities makes us into a new person with a new future. With a banquet of opportunities we put a stop to feeling victimized by circumstance. Our creativity is ramped up as opportunities compel our intellectual and emotional floodgates to open.

At this point, you may be asking, "Why should I put myself through such an intense process?" Normally, our urge with any life problem is to solve it quickly or cover it over. But when it comes to big life stresses and trauma, the Band-Aid approach isn't enough, and denial is a sure path to psychological failure. Without the emotional analysis, meaning, and opportunity that come from all three phases of Recasting, the healing from hurt is usually inadequate and superficial. We may destine ourselves to repeat the same experience. Or we may not emerge from the sadness or depression at all.

As you're about to see in the following cases, Recasting has applications for all of life's greatest stressors and traumas, whether at work, in relationships, or during illness. Sometimes it's the accumulation of what seems like insignificant daily stressors that actually have the most impact. Let's start with a simple example of the kind of everyday stressor we must all deal with if we're to stay in Brilliant Health.

Stories from the Recasting Archives

THE LAUNDRY GODDESS

With four teenagers to raise, Linda spent all day at work, only to return home and toil away her evenings doing laundry in her musty basement, the "dungeon." As much as Linda asked her family to pick up and sort their clothes, there was always Molly's soccer practice, or Aiden's homework, or trips to the supermarket. Helping with the laundry, invariably, came last.

Feelings: "Being stuck down in the dungeon alone was the worst part of my day," says Linda. "I felt such resentment welling up in me night after night. After years of drudgery, little help, and feeling no appreciation, I decided that I had to do something about my anger because I felt tense all the time. And to make matters worse, my bitterness was mixed with a self-induced guilt trip because, after all, isn't a mother supposed to take care of her kids' needs?" As a nurse, Linda recognized anger and guilt as two emotions not conducive to good health.

Meaning: After taking a hard look at the situation and her role in it, new understandings emerged. Her first insight was that she was the one who put herself into this angry state. It was her choice to be angry—and hers alone. Rather than continuing to blame her husband or kids, she decided to focus on the question, "What's my part?" Linda's inquiry prompted new exploration. She concluded that she'd never told her family how much impact this had on her, never had set consequences for her kids' lack of help, and instead had became a shrew, screaming at everyone for any slight infraction even unrelated to laundry. The harsh mood she cast over the household was hurting everyone, and yet, without finding alternatives, she begrudgingly kept doing every load of laundry that came down the chute.

Opportunity: What were the opportunities? As it turned out, there were many. Not only did she come up with possibilities that did more than just eliminate the anger and resentment (her initial goal), to her surprise they ended up enriching her career, her communication with her family, her reputation in the community, and her eventual happiness and health.

Here's what happened: Linda held a family meeting. Gathering the group around a dry-erase board, she calmly shared what she'd been feeling (phase one). Then she revealed new insights about herself (phase two), and lovingly told them she no longer wanted to scream at her loved ones. With marker in hand, she was poised to brainstorm new ideas with the family (phase three). Here are some of the family's innovations:

- Hire a housekeeper.

- Send the laundry out.

- Have a Mom Appreciation Day once a week where the rest of the family would do all the chores.

- Create a Cleanest Clothes Contest for the kids with exciting prizes.

- Move the washer/dryer machines upstairs.

And finally, her thirteen-year-old son, Aiden, declared, "Mom, why don't you become a Laundry Goddess. Turn it into a hobby, 'cause hobbies are fun!!!" The whole family roared with laughter, but Linda was intrigued.

Linda committed to two suggestions, and the family agreed to hold up their end of the bargain by showing more appreciation. "We took our large kitchen pantry and transformed it into a Laundry Sanctuary, and to this day we always refer to it by that name. It's done in bright yellows and oranges. With color-coded sorting bins stashed neatly in cubbyholes, it's a feast for the eyes."

After the room makeover, the second opportunity was to embrace Aiden's proposition and transform herself into the Laundry Goddess. Achieving encyclopedic knowledge of stain management, she became the neighborhood go-to expert for tricky spots and caked-on grime. "If given the chance to list a hobby, I was pleased to say one of mine is laundry. The kids began to point out tricky stain challenges and praised my efforts when I conquered grass stain, motor oil, cranberry juice, and ketchup. As time went on, even dried blood, bubble gum, and ink were defeated in my home. Along with all this laundry bliss came the best parts: my blood pressure's actually down. I feel so much calmer, and I don't yell at the kids as much. And we're closer as a family and share our small frustrations with each other to help find solutions."

Linda now teaches a class for pediatric nurses. The end of the lecture always contains her laundry tips. (Two secrets from Linda: a dash of ammonia will enhance the effectiveness of the detergent, and cheap aerosol hair spray is a solvent for most ink stains.)

It's crucial to deal with situations that take a toll on the body. Though Linda's story is not a dire life circumstance, the daily little stressors can add up and be just as detrimental to our health as a huge trauma. Her story is also important because it shows us that skipping either of the first two phases of Recasting doesn't allow us to properly identify the underlying causes that ultimately point to the real opportunities. Linda's story is a tale about changing stress and anger to invigoration, which also benefited all the members of her family. In allowing them to help her by expressing their opinions, she created stronger bonds. If Linda hadn't aired her dirty emotional laundry and Recast those feelings, she'd still be down in the dungeon and down in the dumps.

Pick a current stressful situation. Start by choosing something manageable. See if you can change your reaction to it by using the Recasting process. First, allow yourself to feel the real emotions around the issue. Second, analyze what it means that you have this problem. Third, what opportunities does this understanding suggest? What actions can you take to change the situation?

Note how you feel once you've moved through all three steps.

Linda used Recasting to find the opportunities in a long-term problem. But there are other uses. A study using our Brilliant Health Research Instrument called HIP-10, found that the ability of cardiovascular patients to Recast is corre-lated with their ability to plan against relapses of their condi-tion. With the help of the Recasting process, we can all learn to identify "Trigger Emotions" early on and head off these negative feelings before they have a chance to take their toll.

RECASTING TRIGGER EMOTIONS

Jayne, who lives in Melbourne, Australia, has been living with multiple sclerosis for many years. When both her parents were killed in an automobile accident, Jayne sank into the depths of de-spondency, which, in turn, triggered a terrible MS flare-up. Even though the loss of one's parents is the kind of experience that can't be erased, Jayne credits Recasting as a major factor in coping.

By repeatedly following the Recasting process, Jayne real-izes that sadness and disappointment always trigger her illness. "The feeling is a deep despair that lodges in my gut. It's a sense of doom washing over my entire body. On holidays, particu-larly Christmas and Mother's Day, or when I see my friends with their parents, the longing is unbearable. Worst of all, that's when my MS gets worse."

When we met Jayne, she explained how Recasting has saved her from this cycle.

Feelings: "I've trained myself. When I first feel the sadness coming on I say, 'Stop, it's time to Recast before I begin to spi-ral down.'"

Meaning: "The meaning can vary. Sometimes it's just realiz-ing that I feel particularly vulnerable right now, or needy, or fatigued. Other times it means that I have to change what I'm doing. Or maybe I have to give myself permission to grieve, and that's OK."

Opportunities: "For me, finding opportunity turns out to be the easiest part. Often the key is converting the sadness into helping someone. At other times, it's immediately focusing on something wonderful that I have in my life, not on the things I don't have. It might be the opportunity to celebrate the wonderful memories I have of my parents.

"The key to the whole thing is allowing the process to move me from one phase to the next so that I'm never stuck in all that despair. This is the secret to managing my disease."

Many of us fall into a pattern in which one specific negative emotion, left unchecked, will mark the beginning of the road to a destructive place. The key is to understand what that sabotaging emotion is and then be aware when it creeps up on us. For some, like Jayne, it's sadness. For many others, anger is most prevalent. For most of us, fear plays a role. Fear is the most primal and powerful emotion. In our centuries of social evolution, it's found many disguises to wear. Hostility, jealousy, hatred, embarrassment, and greed often cover underlying fear.

We frequently work with people like Jayne who are under extreme emotional distress. The emotional pain never really goes away. As traumatic and life-changing as these situations are, getting through them and living with the pain they cause comes down to a fundamental choice. When devastating things happen, you can either learn from them and start to live *more* or become a victim of them and start to live *less*! Unfortunately, there doesn't seem to be a middle road.

We want to share two stories about two men who have, essentially, the same problem. What was particularly interesting about these stories is that we had the chance to talk with these men within days of each other. Their dramatically different outcomes illustrate what can happen with Recasting and what can happen without it.

ZACH: UNPARALYZED BY LIFE

As Zach plunged over a cliff and into a long, fast, uncontrolled roll over an almost vertical field of boulders, he heard his lower back snap. Before he finally stopped, wedged into a deep crevasse high in the Rockies, his medical school training kicked in. "In those seconds of falling, I knew already that I was going to have a lifetime of mobility issues, sexual issues, urinary problems, and relationship trials. I lay there overcome by fear and anger, mostly at myself. Would I be able to move at all? Would pain overcome me? And would my fiancée still marry me?"

Zach's self-diagnosis was correct. In fact, this strapping, athletic, six foot five mountain climber who was in his final year of medical school would be a paraplegic for life. His love of climbing, skiing, and bike riding would go unrealized. And the African adventure he planned after getting his MD would be severely jeopardized.

Feeling: Zach spent months in a rehabilitation facility burning with anger at his own incompetence and fearful that his life would be over. He lay in bed allowing the emotions to wash over him. But the rehab experts forced him to get up and learn new mobility tools: how to get out of bed, lift himself into a wheelchair, and use the bathroom. And while he mastered his physical world, he began a parallel journey of finding meaning in his own life.

Meaning: "First I thought my dreams would come to nothing. But then I realized, to pull through I had to stop being afraid, embrace change, and start learning about my new self. What I learned was that I couldn't rely on my body anymore. I had been strong and capable for my entire life, but that was over. I learned that strength is a mental state, not a physical one, and that emotional resilience is just as powerful as physical resilience if not more so. I learned that pain was just pain, not a disease. I learned that I had become a new person, yet magically I was still the same person. And if I were to get to Africa, my lifelong dream, I'd have to get really creative."

Opportunities: In the face of trauma, Zach found many new prospects. He could plow ahead with medical school, bringing new powers of compassion and insight to the people he would have as patients. He could share his experiences and inspire others. He could nurture and take advantage of the interest his injury stimulated in others and educate them about health and safety. As a clear benefit to his chosen career, he could use his disability to demonstrate that doctors can come in all sizes, shapes, and styles. And he had the opportunity to bring greater sensitivity and newfound gratitude and appreciation to his wife-to-be.

Zach rolled out of medical school in a specially designed wheelchair and was raring to go. Eighteen months after his fall, Zach and his new bride, Amelia, left for Ghana. They would stay and work there for a surprising ten years.

The life-altering Recasting process was a toughening precursor to the mind-bending experiences Zach would have during the next years in the bush lands of Africa. "It was perfect advance training for the deprivations and unexpected complexity of being the first Western doctor in the village. If I had arrived without having dealt with so many personal challenges, I don't think I would have survived. As it was, I came feeling resilient. Amelia and I hitchhiked all over sub-Saharan Africa with the wheelchair. I was carried on the shoulders of tribesmen every morning through the river rapids between my home village and the clinic. And my disability engendered the respect of all the people and helped them heal, too. A local folk saying sprang up: "How can we be sick if the doctor in the rolling chair is well?"

Zach has been home from Ghana for twelve years. Now the Medical Director of a clinic in southern Texas, he treats economically disadvantaged minority patients. Zach describes his life as a "rich mix of personal and professional accomplishments and loving relationships." He visits Africa periodically and has been spotted recently in the rain forests of Costa Rica.

Does Zach wish he'd never plunged over that cliff? Absolutely. Does he sometimes have days of sadness and feelings of victimhood? Yes. Yet Recasting pulls him through. He's convinced the accident has been an incredible teacher, informing his life more powerfully than any of his other experiences.

What happens when the Recasting process is broken? Meet Derek.

DEREK: PARALYZED BY LIFE

At thirty-two, Derek was a sports enthusiast who craved a good adrenaline rush. Like Zach, his love of vigorous outdoor activity was where he got his joy. On a picture-perfect day at the coastal cliffs just north of San Diego, Derek and his single-surface hang glider soared over sand and sea. But a wayward gust caught his wings, cartwheeled the hang glider, and slammed it against the jagged cliffs. The impact and fall left Derek a lifelong paraplegic.

"The happy man I knew went away that day," mourned ex-wife, Christine. Unlike Zach, Derek has remained a bitter man for the last twenty years. Rather than acknowledging feelings and using them to direct his healing, the bitterness drove him to increasing misery and unaccountability with each passing year. He never lifted out of the lower brain and ended up continually reliving the initial pain and trauma as the victim. The accident became his excuse for giving up on life and for making unhealthy choices: overeating, driving up cholesterol levels, and drinking too much. Hanging onto anger was Derek's downfall, rendering him increasingly psychologically and physically weak. Emotionally numb, he is now divorced and has barely maintained contact with his two sons.

If we analyze Zach and Derek, here's what emerges: two men with close to the same physical condition, yet two extremely different quality-of-life outcomes. Being in their presence, you easily see it. Shrunken in the wheelchair, Derek's belief that "the horrible event ruined my life," has made the statement a self-fulfilling truth. But spend an afternoon with Zach, as we did, and you can't help but feel energized and inspired by this vibrant, powerful man who has recast himself as incredibly accomplished, capable, and healthy. And he is.

The dynamic synergy between Brilliant Health's first five practices is illustrated by Zach's story. His *intention* to reclaim a happy life overrides his anger and fear. He's highly *accountable*, staying away from victimhood as he forges through medical school with determination and discipline. Zach *identifies* his greatest passions and begins to envision himself thriving in Africa. His *centrality* of adventure and outdoor experience lead him to fulfillment in Ghana. And, by *recasting*, Zach puts himself in the physical and mental condition to live his dreams, in spite of the physical odds.

Sometimes, another of the Brilliant Health practices is a companion to successful Recasting. In the next story, it turns out to be Centrality.

SEND IN THE CLOWNS

At age nineteen, Trudi was diagnosed with fast-growing non-Hodgkin's lymphoma. The next two and a half years of radiation and chemo were, she says, hellish. Although she was unaware of Recasting per se, over time that's precisely what she did.

Feelings: "I was so exhausted I could hardly move, and I was isolated from all the things I loved to do: hanging out with friends, telling stories, and being the class clown. Everything you do as a normal kid had been ripped away from me. I didn't pay that much attention to what I felt at the time, but now I see I was very angry."

Trudi's attempts to come to grips with her situation were a naive phase one of the Recasting process. Certainly, she wasn't consciously crafting how she was responding, but nonetheless, her anger evoked a greater clarity about what she needed to do and who she wanted to be. What did she see? Phase two opened up in front of her.

Meaning: Trudi continued, "During that long period of disability something happened. Tiny fissures opened that gave me a look into my own heart. I think this was uncommon for a teenager. It's odd. In a way I was lucky.

"Up until then, every part of my body was under the control of someone or something other than me: the doctors, the treatments, the medications. The insight that changed everything was, in order to feel empowered, I had to ditch the anger and take whatever control I could over my body and my life."

Opportunity: Trudi fought to reach a point where some activity was possible. What would make her feel most powerful, effective, and alive? Intuitively, she knew it was her number one Centrality: performing. The forced inactivity had only proved to her just how much she enjoyed hamming it up in front of others.

"Nothing will stop a born actor. The first day I could leave the house, my fantasies became realities. I enrolled in acting class at the junior college. I was like a madwoman, performing anywhere I could find an audience. Within a couple of months I was out on the streets doing a mime act. The more people I could attract, the more alive I felt. I loved it.

"Looking around, I noticed that jugglers made the most money. Even though I was still taking anticancer treatments, I applied to clown school and was accepted."

Three years after her last chemo session, Trudi received an offer to be a professional clown in an internationally known circus. That's where she met the love of her life, fellow clown and now husband, Rusty.

Twenty years later, Trudi remains healthy. What does she say about the process she now knows as Recasting?

"It was a slow, incremental journey of discovering my authentic self and how I could express it. The anger and frustration led me to recognize what I needed, and that recognition moved me to action that opened up new ways to live. Without the disease, I'd never have taken the risk to perform on city street corners or become a professional clown."

There are various ways to use Recasting. It can be a completely internal process that moves you from one phase to the next, or it can be useful to get a trusted friend to help. In our workshops, people frequently tell us that Recasting with others gives them a way to verbalize a problem, get validation that some of the opportunities are good ideas, and, because we may be blind to the route out of our own problems, get an objective view. It's also a way of bringing fresh energy to a personal problem. We've often had people leave our sessions on a complete high, full of relief, and excited to try some of the new opportunities they've uncovered.

A recent study using the Brilliant Health model finds a significant correlation between our ability to Recast and a perception of good health. It's no wonder. It feels good to resolve a painful problem. We feel stronger and more capable.

If you're dealing with a serious illness, disability, or trauma, we suggest you take yourself through all three steps of Recasting. However, you need to be aware of the time element. Recasting can take place quickly, but the more serious the problem, the more time you may need to work it through. Sometimes it can take weeks, or months, or much longer. Be gentle with yourself. Ask for help from friends. Remember that creating new patterns of behavior and response happens with practice.

By following the three phases of Recasting, we're much more able to cope with negative feelings, giving us a sense of pride in our ability to handle whatever life throws our way. And Recasting gives us the self-confidence to know that the next time we make a mistake or hit a major crisis, life won't come crashing down around us.

While Recasting empowers us with a sense of our own capabilities, the next Brilliant Health practice allows you to look at your own life with a sense of hope.

Life is not what it's supposed to be. It's what it is. The way you cope with it is what makes the difference.

—VIRGINIA SATIR (1916–1988),

American psychologist

Options

*Prepare yourself for the world, as the [Grecian] athletes used
to do for their exercise; oil your mind and your manners, to
give them the necessary suppleness and flexibility; strength
alone will not do.*

—THE EARL OF CHESTERFIELD (1694–1773)

Some time around the year 500 BCE, Lao-tzu, father of Tao-
ism, said, "Whatever is flexible and loving will tend to grow;
whatever is rigid and blocked will wither and die." This is especially true when it comes to Brilliant Health. Throughout
human history, flexibility and its many synonyms—suppleness,
stretch, elasticity, openness, bounce, flow—have been descrip-
tors of growth and good health. These words are also the source
of creativity, innovation, and problem solving. At the other end
of the continuum, words associated with rigidity and limited
possibilities describe ill health and demise: stiff, uncompromis-
ing, frozen, unbending, stuck.

What Lao-tzu intuitively knew and modern-day scientists
are only now beginning to fully understand is that flexible
thinking and opening up options sends the brain into a higher
plane and makes our bodies work better. As we learned in the

Intention chapter, it is flexible thought and innovative behaviors that clear the furrows in our neural pathways.

The sixth Brilliant Health practice is Options, with which you create hope, resilience, and a high quality of life by generating new possibilities.

Opening up options is just plain fun. When we lead sessions on innovation with groups of people, and they start to realize how many more options they have, there's a palpable energy boost in the room. As people come up with new approaches to old problems, they become more animated, the vocal volume in the room soars, there's laughter even when the topic is serious, and everyone is engaged in the process. What we're witnessing in these sessions is the excitement generated when people begin to see the possibility of something better. Once again, medical research helps us understand why.

Studies show that opening up new options leads to positive emotions and optimism, which have healthy biochemical and energetic effects. Specifically, they reveal that optimistic patients return to activity sooner after surgery. Plus their coronary arteries are more resistant to the development of dangerous thickenings, and their offspring are born with healthier birth weights. On the other hand, feeling stuck is associated with pessimism, which one animal research study called *learned helplessness*. When lab animals are subjected to stress over which they have no control, they have strong physical responses. Over time, the poor critters learn to be helpless, close down emotionally, and have heightened responses to future stresses because they've learned it's futile to look for alternatives or escape. This is a pattern frequently seen in humans who have experienced highly traumatic events in childhood or adulthood.

Hope

When we don't have options, we don't have hope. And we need hope. It's proven to help us cope with illness and trauma. A hospice care doctor we know summed it up this way: "If there's one thing I've learned over the last thirty years, it's that right down to someone's last breath you never, ever take away the feeling of hope."

Can people on their deathbeds live in Brilliant Health and have hope? Yes. But it's a different kind of hope than most of us would think. Their hope is not about the disease going away or about having a considerable extension on their life. Rather, patients with end-stage disease say they hope to "avert further suffering," "live life to its fullest in whatever time they have left," or that their "families have a better future." These hopes aren't illusory; they're achievable, arising from the ability to foresee realistic and life-affirming possibilities. Even when their own death is well within their sight, these patients have found options and created hope, allowing themselves peace at the end of life, deeper connections with their families, and choices about the quality of their remaining days.

Consider what options you have left unexplored. Start somewhere you feel stuck or trapped. Are there new paths that will take you into happier territory? Note how you feel when you're considering possibilities. And note your physical and emotional reactions when you find a new route.

How Do You Spell Stress? With Four *F*'s!

You may be familiar with the two arms of the stress response named *fight* and *flight*, each of which ramps up our bodies for the ultimate survival response. But now scientists have extended their description of stress reactions to include two more: *fright* and *freeze*. All four are in evidence throughout the animal kingdom, and are evolutionarily designed to save us from immediate physical danger.

Yet unlike most animals, stress for humans is not so much about actual physical danger, it's about social behavior. Your most recent stress reactions, like rapid breathing, shakiness, and increased heart rate, were likely to be your response to speaking in public or an argument.

We've all seen people respond physically to social stressors. Picture someone you know who always resorts to *fight* or preemptive attack when cornered. Envision someone who responds with *flight*, running away from any potential conflict. Think about the person who instantly *freezes*, and becomes incapable of any decision or action. Or, consider the *frightened* person in a constant state of anxiety, worry, and fear. These are all powerful, biochemically compelling responses, but what saved us from physical attack in prehistoric times is a driving cause of all our modern stress-related illnesses.

Lucky for us, using our higher-brain, we've found innovative ways to respond to old threats. We can access and harness the higher-brain functions by opening the doors to different Options. As soon as we're aware of our reactive response to an emotional trauma, conflict, or illness—anything that is capable of triggering the Four *F*'s—we can begin to engage these higher brain powers.

This is not to suggest that the route out of fear magically arrives with the snap of your fingers. Sometimes it can take considerable time and practice to overcome our four-*F* responses to childhood abuse, frightening adult relationships, or a life-threatening illness. But opening Options over time, seeing new possibilities, and creating new ways to respond are all flexible behaviors capable of establishing new neural pathways out of the traumatic emotions.

> Do you tend toward one of the four *F*'s (*fight, flight, fright,* and *freeze*)? Identify a situation in the past in which you responded with it. Then look for options and opportunities that might have allowed you to respond differently.

Thriving

One rule for thriving comes down to a fundamental thought. And that thought, the secret to flourishing, prospering, booming, and blooming, is revealed in three words we heard half a world away.

THREE UNFORGETTABLE WORDS

When Greg was interviewing in the stunningly beautiful country of Vietnam, he was taken to an orphanage housing three hundred indigent children from infancy to sixteen years of age. It was a broken-down, overcrowded building in one of the poorest sections of Ho Chi Minh City. The diminutive and remarkable woman who runs the orphanage is Su Nu Tri. Through a translator, Greg learned that many of the children arrive physically or emotionally unhealthy and without any possessions.

Faced with the overwhelming obstacles of being orphaned and impoverished, Greg asked Su Nu Tri, "Can you tell which children will thrive, that is, go on to be healthy and productive?" Greg prepared for a long pause while she considered his question. But in a split-second response, Su Nu Tri uttered three unforgettable words: "Yes," she said, "They see possibilities!"

Why is her response so important for all of us? Because this woman, having raised thousands of children, can see that the best indicator for success is the child's ability to see options. Even though the kids who thrive have nothing in a material sense, they simply don't see limitations. These special children envision a life far beyond their current reality optimistically, and they assume they can go on to be or do anything. Greg could easily identify these kids, because they were the ones bubbling with questions, inquisitive about other people and cultures, and willing to participate in any new challenge or opportunity. For them, the ability to open options can trump the grinding disadvantages that come with poverty.

The story suggests we can all thrive, too. When we uncover multiple possibilities, we feel the exhilaration that comes from believing we're capable of creating anything for ourselves.

DIVERGENT PATHS

Su Nu Tri's thoughts have become a mantra for the two of us. In our lives, these three words translate into an urge to open options by creating divergent paths, rather than setting goals with benchmarks and specific outcomes. In fact, these days, our only goal is to have no goals.

Let's face it, our society is goal-oriented. Yet, inflexible and unalterable goals tend to lock us into specific outcomes and act as blinders to keep us from being distracted by the wide variety of possibilities life throws our way. We realized in our happiness research that locking into rigid assumptions of how things *should* go rarely delivers what any of us really wanted in the first place. And when we don't achieve our tangible goal, we can end up feeling like failures. The truth is, we don't find the real happiness and quality of life we crave by only focusing on the personal goals we set, like losing thirty pounds, getting a better relationship, a bigger house, or a promotion.

Even when we reach these goals, they give us only a fleeting feeling of satisfaction. A sustained, happy life isn't created by a major achievement or by making a large purchase. Rather, it occurs incrementally, through delightful moment-to-moment explorations.

Self-Limiting Beliefs

If we have an Options wish for you, it's to not give in to your limiting beliefs. Self-limiting beliefs tend to show up when you decide to experience something new. They present themselves in internal statements like, "It probably won't work." "I'm not good at it." "What if my efforts don't lead to anything?" "I don't know how to do it." "I'll look like a fool." All of these thoughts run contrary to action and progress. It's like backing your car out of the driveway in hope of going on a trip, and then driving right back into the garage. If you want your physical, intellectual, or emotional travels to be far-flung and wide-ranging, you'll have to leave the self-limiting beliefs at home.

> Here's our challenge to you. Find a way to create an adventure. Push yourself to do something you've kept under wraps because of self-limiting beliefs. If you never thought you were good at art, take a painting class. If you're a city person, go on a rigorous guided hike in the mountains. If take-out cuisine is your thing, prepare a gourmet dinner for friends. It's not about being successful the first time out. Push yourself to expand your concept of yourself. Most of all, it's about not capitulating to those self-limiting beliefs.

THE MARTHA

To give you an example of what we're talking about, we'll share an escapade in which our own self-limiting beliefs threatened one of our most enjoyable endeavors.

One day the two of us decided to fix up an abandoned rowboat in the Berkeley Marina, known by the locals as *The Martha*. We bought some supplies, like a few cans of bright yellow paint, pulled her out of the water, scraped off years of barnacles, and began to lay on the first strokes of color. One by one, Rick's houseboat neighbors came by, each with the same response: "Is that *The Martha*? She looks beautiful! But, didn't you know? *The Martha* is mine!"

After we finished our restoration and took out the newly gleaming *Martha* for her first spin, she became the hottest little boat in the marina. Everyone began to fight over her. These events, and the ones that ensued, took on the makings of a story full of colorful characters, greed, community fighting, false blame, an unsolved mystery, heroics, and, finally, celebration.

One of our core intentions is creating new adventures, so in the wake of the *Martha* incident, we looked at each other and said, "Hey, want to write a children's book?" And so we did. But not before having to conquer some self-limiting beliefs that could have sunk the project before it ever started. "Do we have the time, skill, energy, and financial resources to take this on?" we wondered. There were other potential pitfalls. "With our own children in their twenties, do we even know what little kids like?" and "What will we do with it when we finish?" We didn't know the answers to these questions, but we took a leap of faith. Pushing ourselves to not worry about the end result, we set some intentions for the project: to have fun, to be stimulated, to be creative, and to learn new things.

We wrote our first draft and put together our book specifications, and gave them to our literary agent, who found an interested publisher. The publisher told us, "I like your idea, but it won't sell. Lose all the rhyme, change the book from a true story to fiction, forget the unsophisticated look of watercolors. Computerized art is the way we do it now."

Suddenly our project was saddled with outside mandates that threatened to stop it from being fun, stimulating, and creative. Each one of our intentions was being killed off by the realities of the publishing industry. So we decided to say, "No thanks," and open up a radical new option. We started our own publishing company.

We then dove into areas that intrigued us but that we never imagined we'd experience. We were over our heads in art and illustrators, lyrical writing, layout, graphic design, printing, publishing, and hawking a children's book at publisher's fairs. The finished product, *The Martha Is Mine*, is everything we wanted it to be: a rhyming, vividly bright, watercolor-filled picture book, telling an almost true story.

How is the *Martha* adventure related to Brilliant Health? Delight is contagious. What we learned from this experience is that if you go with what delights you, and you don't let yourself be halted by any roadblocks, and you prompt yourself to explore your options, the very process itself perpetuates the joy that got you started.

Our experience with the *Martha* provided us with something that's now discussed frequently in research studies: variety. Something that initially provides great pleasure loses its power with repetition. Our human systems need newness to maintain happiness over time, and that means adding new experiences to our lives. Brilliant Health is enhanced by diversity, surprise, unexpected adventure, and breaks from sameness, even if that sameness is pleasant.

The idea of sameness provided Rita, in our next story, with great comfort until something threw her off course.

PLAYING IT SAFE ISN'T SAFE

Rita's life had been pleasant, well-planned, predictable, stable, and secure. Of all the things she was afraid of, the thought of death petrified her the most. So she committed to regular exercise, a consistent diet, and doing everything else in moderation as a technique to deal with that fear. She carried this regularity into every aspect of her life. For twenty-six years, Rita had worked at the same school and lived in the same house. She shopped in the same stores, walked the same routes, and hung out with the same people. It felt safe.

To tell the whole of Rita's story, however, we need to take you back to a particular time five years ago, to what should have been a fun-filled family vacation. "In one day I went from perceiving myself as the healthiest person I knew," she recalls, "to having a life-threatening disease. This was quite a blow to someone with fears of both change and death."

While skiing in the Sierra Nevada backcountry, Rita noticed it was difficult to catch her breath. "Maybe I've had too much wine," she thought. "Or, maybe I don't adjust to altitude like I used to." That evening in the hotel gym she felt a piercing stab in her chest but dismissed it. After all, fifty-five-year-old Rita had done everything to stay healthy.

But things got worse. A trip to the hospital and an angiogram showed that she'd had a serious heart attack and evidence of an already-damaged heart. Despite the fact that cardiologists opened a blocked artery with a stent, for the next four and half months Rita continued to decline, at times feeling the horror of her body slipping away from life. When the doctors performed surgery again, they were surprised to find additional serious occlusions. At this point, emergency triple bypass surgery was performed, during which Rita came close to death. And, to make matters even more distressing, a new wrench was thrown into Rita's medical story. Doctors diagnosed her cardiovascular illness as a rare genetic disorder.

Even with a genetic condition hanging over her head, during the next few months, Rita's lifelong fear of death began to lessen. Confronting it face-to-face led to an epiphany. "I came so close to dying that I actually saw the white lights. And it wasn't all that bad. Because I got that close, death was demystified. This rocked my world. I felt a freedom from the fear of death for the first time in my life."

The word *freedom* is synonymous with *options*. Rita's freedom from fear enabled her to abandon the regularity she felt was protection against death. Within the person who had been carefully treading the well-worn and predictable path of her life, Rita discovered an experimental, joyful, flexible woman: herself! Filled with new feelings of wild abandon, power, and free rein, she ventured beyond the borders of her previous experience.

"My life is ten times better, because baby, now I try it all. Everywhere I look, there are new prospects lying in wait. I used to think, 'Wow, there are amazing people out there who travel the world, write books, act in theaters, and start their own companies.' These days I pinch myself every morning because I'm one of those people!"

Here's a thumbnail sketch of her life since ending her twenty-six-year tenure as a special education teacher. She:

- Mentors kids a half day a week.

- Facilitates an Equity Program for children that she developed.

- Consults on educational strategies for second-language students around the country.

- Performs the one-woman show she wrote about her brush with death.

- Writes a series of novels for teenagers from other countries who are newly arrived in the United States.

- Serves on the board of an organization that helps disenfranchised kids.

- Works with an Ethiopian woman who is writing a book about her country.

- Travels to Guatemala every summer to learn Spanish and work with kids in a Mayan school.

Rita's story can teach us a great deal. Let's not wait until we have a near-death experience to live richly, to do what we most want to do, to grab the golden ring of adventure. Feeling paralyzed in the grip of fear keeps us in the deeply emotional, physical stress response zone. And if we remain unaware of this, we suffer all of its negative consequences. This is a dark side of our primitive brains, the lower brain's ability to suck us down into the quicksand of an emotional swamp and keep us trapped there.

OPTIONS IN THE HOLY LAND

Expansion takes place in many forms. As Americans, we tend to think of adventure, or what in this book we call Options, in terms of traveling to unfamiliar places, experiencing new things, and doing things in a different way. But even as we have journeyed all over the world, we've learned that physical travel isn't necessarily a requirement for finding Options. In fact, very often, opening options can take place without ever having to go anywhere. It happens within.

We ran into this quite unexpectedly while wandering through a crowded bazaar in Jerusalem. We came to a tiny store of nine feet by fourteen, one of many in the teeming shopping area. Every inch of this stall was filled with jewelry, antiques, and artifacts. Our senses were overwhelmed by the sheer amount of things in that cramped space. We saw gleaming gold and silver necklaces, bracelets, earrings, and watches. Mixed in was an equally intriguing assortment of antiques, old military medals, and pocket watches. There was a dizzying array of colorful beads, bags, textiles, and countless other curiosities. But the most fascinating find in that tiny stall was the men who ran it: two brothers, Abdullah and Mohamed. They welcomed us into their crowded shop, offering us tea and telling us that they had been working together in that space, side by side, from dawn to dusk, six days a week, since 1949.

It's hard to imagine any two people being happy in such a seemingly constrained environment, but Abdullah and Mohamed are everything but constrained. These brothers, both in their late seventies, are endearingly sweet-tempered and amazingly energetic. Like the countless items in their shop, they shine with color and vibrancy. Abdullah and Mohamed haven't traveled much in their lives. They don't have to. They're enthralled with the world that comes into their shop each day. Not only do they read three daily newspapers and revel in the conversation of their many friends and neighbors, they solicit stories from each person they meet. "Every new customer is the chance for learning, expanding our minds and opinions," they told us. "We get to travel the world with the tourists who come into our shop."

Abdullah and Mohamed remind us that our physical environments don't have to define who we are or set limits on how we live. No matter who you are or what physical limitations you face, you can have an internal life that is unrestrained, intellectually welcoming, and flexible.

WHEN RIGIDITY CAN KILL

Whether we're in a nine-by-fourteen-foot-shop by choice or trapped in a nine-by-fourteen-foot prison cell, there are always more options than we think there are. Always. We can't ever underestimate that fact. If we do, we shut down the brain, our thinking becomes meager, and as is the case with Carmen, we risk consigning ourselves to a dangerous life sentence.

Carmen moved to Oregon to join her fiancé, Ned, whom she'd met when both were on business trips to New York. It was a bold move because, other than Ned, Carmen had no support system or job. When she discovered a tiny lump in her breast, she went into panic mode. Without medical insurance, the cost of medical testing and possible hospitalizations would bankrupt her new relationship. Since Carmen and her fiancé believed they had no other options, they made a self-limiting assumption. Descending into a depressed deep freeze, they locked into what they thought was their only plan: to marry in a quick ceremony, wait the obligatory three months for Ned's medical insurance to go into effect, and then visit the doctor. To protect their scheme, they shared it with no one, including their families.

When the insurance kicked in and doctors finally did an examination, the tumor had grown to four centimeters, and cancer cells were found in the surrounding lymph nodes. After three months of waiting in chronic fear and panic over the unknown, Carmen now had confirmation that she was facing an aggressive cancer.

The relationship between creating options and all rungs on the Brilliant Health staircase becomes obvious in the tragedy of Carmen's story. Those three months of chronic depression and fear led her to inaction, poor decisions, and disaffection from her family. And even worse, her deep fear and panic may have dulled her immune system's ability to perform essential surveillance and eradication of cancer cells.

In retrospect, there were many options she could have taken. Her community was more than sufficiently serviced by free clinics, women's health centers, and support groups. And Ned's loving family who, in fact, had the ample emotional and financial resources to help at an earlier stage, was left hurt, alienated, and afraid.

There are very few instances where inaction could kill us. For most of us, our readiness factor needs to activate before we go into high gear. But in all circumstances, ongoing investigation of possibilities is a prelude to richer, better-informed solutions.

JACKIE BREAKS INTO THE LIGHT

At thirty-nine, Jackie was diagnosed with lupus, a condition in which the immune system attacks the body's cells and tissues. Her energy was zapped, and it was frequently hard just to get to work. She felt chained to every part of her life: the musty apartment, Brooklyn's chilly winters and humid summers, and the lack of nature around her.

When we began working with Jackie, we realized that she was unable, or perhaps unwilling, to consider options and break free. Every possible solution our support group presented to her was met with a limiting belief as to why she couldn't do it. Where could she open up new avenues, new ways of doing things, live differently? How might she be less depressed, even happy? Jackie could provide no answers. Yet somehow, some deep, opaque urge kept Jackie coming to Brilliant Health workshops month after month.

To our surprise, in month number nine of the workshop, Jackie got it. Everything opened up. She started seeing herself running alongside a dog in the countryside. A deep yearning for warmer climates, blue skies, and daytime jaunts took over. Jackie's readiness factor had kicked in.

In just over a month, Jackie emptied her fourth-floor walk-up apartment, investigated until she found a new team of doctors in Dallas, and hit the road with her new puppy. Her report back to the Brilliant Health group was happy. Though her health prognosis was still uncertain, she no longer felt doomed.

Breaking the Chains

Jackie exemplified an issue we must all consider. If what you've been doing and where you've been living has brought you to an unhealthy state of stress, depression, disease, or disability, you have to do everything in your power to change those circumstances, both internally and externally. We've heard countless stories of people who've made spontaneous recoveries from diseases with horrendous prognoses. Often, their changes were extreme. Whether it was a radical change of diet, lifestyle, thought patterns, jobs, or relationships, they altered their environment sufficiently to create drastic changes in their internal chemistry.

Two Roads: Which Will You Take?

There are two highways of life. There's the interstate: the direct, point-A-to-Z approach that values the known roadway for its efficiency and comfort. And then there's the rural route with its unexpected detours and delightful investigations along the way. The first may feel most effective, but staying on it exclusively could create a limited life. The second route is marked by variety, the unexpected, experimentation, hope, and flexibility. Given a choice, Brilliantly Healthy people drive both routes. But, deep in their hearts, they particularly love to drive the back roads, believing that just getting to the destination is not nearly as exhilarating as enjoying the process along the way.

Options

I always wanted a happy ending . . . now I've learned, the hard way, that some poems don't rhyme, and some stories don't have a clear beginning, middle, and end. Life is about not knowing, having to change, taking the moment and making the best of it without knowing what's going to happen next. Delicious ambiguity.

—GILDA RADNER (1946–1989)

SEVEN

Appreciation

*Keeping your body healthy is an expression of gratitude to
the whole cosmos—the trees, the clouds, everything.*

—THICH NHAT HANH (1926–)

Spend ten seconds reveling in what you appreciate, and you can emerge with a new perspective, feel energized, and reset your body. A few simple words of expressed appreciation can transform a worrisome problem, break down walls between you and others, and create a domino effect of goodwill that spreads throughout an entire community.

Gratitude is being thankful for the bounty of life, and Brilliant Health Appreciation is the most active and deepest form of being grateful. It's a rich understanding and expression of the meaning, quality, and importance of our lives, our bodies, and our own incredible multidimensional selves. This intense recognition leads to feeling worthwhile, valuable, and in control.

When we first started interviewing happy people, we were bowled over with the sheer volume of Appreciation we heard.

They didn't just tend toward Appreciation, they were completely committed to it. Our discussions were continually interrupted midsentence with, "Oh, it's so wonderful you're here." "I want you to know how much I'm enjoying our discussion." "Did you notice how blue the sky is today?" "Look at those beautiful begonias . . ." and on and on and on. The two of us began to refer to these break-ins as "Appreciation time-outs" and would give each other a knowing nod whenever the next one occurred. But this was only the beginning of the lengths they'd go. Once back home, we were inundated with emails, faxed notes, and even Hallmark cards thanking us for our visits.

At first we made the naive assumption that happy people were just an inherently grateful bunch, at times bordering on what we thought was syrupy sweetness. Certainly it was a way to see the glass as half-full, but there appeared to be more to it. Additional inquiries and closer analysis finally revealed its hidden effects. Being in a state of deep Appreciation is a surefire way to keep us rooted in the present.

Now, after years of facilitating Appreciation exercises, we're convinced that when you're in the act of appreciating someone, something, or yourself, all worries about the past and anxieties about the future evaporate. You're only attuned to what is good in the here and now. And that's a great place to be. A common thread of multiple world philosophies and religions is the profound value of being in the moment or fully present.

It's no wonder that presence is so important and makes us feel healthy. In its most primary and ancient form, being present made us aware of what we needed to best survive. It was about being present with other members of your clan, and awareness of potential threats and possibilities for food and water. In our modern era, being in the present offers momentary freedom from worry and stress and all the physical hurt that comes with them. When we actively appreciate, the world feels right. We're calm and energized at the same time. Being in this state gives us the pause and respite to reset our bodies to focus on what is good and nonthreatening. This allows our parasympathetic nervous system to kick in, focusing on *relax and restore*, the opposite functions of *fight or flight*.

The two of us have gone from thinking of constant Appreciation as somewhat sappy to believing in its great force. Now we're both rigorously committed to doing our own Appreciation time-outs. It feels wonderful to acknowledge when great things are happening. But, almost more important, Appreciation time-outs are essential when things aren't going so well. The momentarily frustrating situation is often brightened by a blast of Appreciation for the things that are good in our lives.

Once each day, set your watch to go off at a certain time—let's say two o'clock in the afternoon. Regardless of what you're doing, direct your mind to something you can appreciate about that moment. It might be the fact that you live in a beautiful climate, you're surrounded by people you love, or you have the opportunity to be a parent. Watch what happens to your body and your sense of wellness.

The Appreciative Brain

Appreciation takes advantage of something we've mentioned before: the brain's attention deficit, a natural limitation that allows it to focus fully on only one thing at a time. When we appreciate, we're highlighting the positive, making our brain less able to focus on pain and negative experiences. Appreciation practice is a cognitive and behavioral strategy that makes us more adaptive to life experiences. It's protective against depression and being emotionally stuck after a traumatic experience. In fact, war veterans who engaged in Appreciation were less likely to suffer from the symptoms of post-traumatic stress disorder.

One study revealed some dramatic results about what happens when we're in a state of appreciation. It divided several hundred people into three groups: the first kept a diary accounting for everything that occurred during each day, a second group kept a diary of only unpleasant experiences, and the third recorded only things for which they were grateful.

The results of the study showed that the "gratitude group" reported higher levels of alertness, enthusiasm, determination, optimism, and energy, and experienced less depression and stress. They were also more likely to help others and to feel loved.

In this chapter, we'll share how you can capitalize on the three aspects of Brilliant Health Appreciation: valuing life, valuing yourself, and expressing appreciation to others.

Valuing Life

When our Vietnamese guide and interpreter took us to the Old People's Center on the banks of the Saigon River in Ho Chi Minh City, we asked its director two questions: "Who's the happiest person here, and who's the healthiest person here?" "Oh, that's easy," he said. "The answer to both questions is the same: her name is Ba Tham."

We were brought to meet the eighty-two-year-old Ba Tham, an animated and colorful character with an absolutely glowing smile.

"We hear you're happy," we said. "Oh yes," she replied. "I'm so happy."

To understand the power of her story, we'll give you a glimpse into Ba Tham's history. During the Vietnam War she was kidnapped by the South Vietnamese and forced into prostitution. As a prostitute she was required to act as a spy against the Viet Cong. Ba Tham was told if she didn't obey their orders, she'd never see her husband and five children again. Horrified by that possibility, she did as they said.

During the war, Ba Tham's legs were tragically mangled in a bombing raid. And, when the war was over, she learned that her husband and three of her children had been killed. To her sorrow, the two living children refused to have anything to do with her because of the stigma of prostitution.

Eventually Ba Tham found her way to the Center, a crumbling shack nearly falling into the river. Moving around only with the assistance of others, she now spends most of her days immobile on a cot next to a modest bundle containing her worldly belongings.

Greg was eager to ask Ba Tham the obvious question: "Why are you so happy?" Her reply: "Because I have *so much.*" To our eyes it was not apparent that she had anything at all. "What do you have?" Greg asked.

Ba Tham beamed, "I have my favorite birds that sing outside my window; the chanting from the temple; my friends who come by each day to visit; my little book of paper for drawing; the colors in the trees, the breeze from the river. I have so much."

Ba Tham's appreciation of abundance when she seemed to have so little is a striking contrast to so many of us who feel empty when we have so much. It's easy to take for granted the simplest yet most important things in our world. Ba Tham's story offers a compelling contrast to those times when we're seduced into finding what's wrong or missing from our lives. A what-I-don't-have mind-set directs us to unhappiness. Yet, just like Ba Tham, regardless of our material resources, we all have so much to appreciate: the capacity to love, to feel deeply, the sun, the air to breathe, loving friends, eyes to see, and ears to hear the glorious sights and sounds all around us.

BEYOND SURVIVING, TO THRIVING

Ba Tham's deep Appreciation is similar to some of the people we've worked with in support groups for people who've been treated for aggressive cancers. Particularly illustrative is the experience of survivors one year out from treatment. The true thrivers, the ones who aggressively Recast their illness and forge ahead with exuberance, seem to gravitate in two healthy directions. First, they become Options masters and decide to open up their life to a bounty of adventure. Second, they become mega-appreciative of being alive. With this high level of Appreciation, they then use laser-sharp emotional radar to determine what's best and most valuable in their lives.

FRACTURED FLUFF

Cheryl is in remission from a cancer that has a fifty-fifty chance of recurrence. She's only recently returned to her job as manager of a large insurance company. "I've become very pragmatic about what's important in my life," she told us. "Postcancer, what I really care about and appreciate is so crystal clear that it's easier to make decisions. The difference is most dramatic at work, where I used to be overwhelmed by petty politics and manipulative comments. Precancer, I'd come home at the end of the day and compulsively replay each discussion, thinking, 'I should have said this or that.' I'd dissect people's words and plan my next-day response. Now I filter right on the spot. I call it 'fractured fluff.' If I even start to go down that path, I laugh and say, 'I'm not putting my energy there. I'm staying in appreciation of my life.'"

But how do we appreciate in a world of pain?

OVERRIDING HURT

Margie fights ichthyosis, a rare genetic disorder that causes the skin to turn to fishlike scales. Flare-ups are extremely painful and unsightly, and strong histamine responses cause Margie's moods to plummet. "Each episode left me angry and feeling sorry for myself. I'd be so defeated that I'd adopt an I-don't-care-anymore attitude and resort to unhealthy ways of comforting myself. I'd overspend on clothes, drink too much, and eat everything in sight. When I felt sorry for myself, I'd put all my attention on what was wrong with my life." In doing so, Margie was unwittingly pulling herself down the staircase of health. In the process, she unknowingly lowered her threshold for pain, and more pain led her to be more negative.

"One day, after landing a big account at work, I felt so pleased with myself and grateful for the help of my colleagues. Suddenly, I noticed that the pain wasn't as bad. I put two and two together. Using Appreciation as an antidote was a great personal discovery. Now, when an episode occurs, I turn my attention to the incredible blessings in my life. That works better than anything else at cutting the pain and the emotional suffering that comes with it. I'm proud to tell people that Appreciation is my new drug of choice."

Margie's insight applies to any time we feel down, lonely, scared, anxious, run-down, defeated, or powerless. Instead of turning to unhealthy self-medication or addiction, we can turn to the self-enhancing alternative that's always available: deep appreciation.

A TRIP TO THE DOCTOR

The morning of getting the news of his third prostate biopsy in six years, Rick was extremely anxious. His PSA scores were high, and there was a family history of prostate cancer. "I worked the Brilliant Health model on myself. I was able to contain the tension to some degree by setting an intention to be calm and focused. But by the time the nurse escorted me to the examining room, my heart was pounding, I was sweating, and my mind was racing. This could easily be one of those terrible bits of news that would forever change my life. I was anything but focused. Then the nurse popped her head in and told me the doctor would be delayed by another fifteen minutes. I said to myself, 'OK, Rick, you're a happiness consultant, what would you tell someone else to do?' My answer was: 'Appreciate this moment, and do it quickly!' "

What was there to appreciate in a small, windowless alcove? As it turned out there were many things: "The high quality of my doctor; that I can afford good insurance; that I have access to excellent medical care; the modern equipment in the room; the fact that, if I had cancer, it would likely be an 'early catch'; my loving support system who would be there for me unconditionally."

By the time the doctor strolled in, Rick was much more present, calm, cool, and collected. The news was good, and with his wits about him, he was able to hear the diagnosis and ask intelligent questions about managing his health as he moved forward. He could relax and enjoy this unusual moment.

Appreciating Yourself

Some of us already make it a practice to appreciate the external world around us. But we don't do as well at self-appreciation. Though our culture supports appreciating the people and the world around us, there are strong cultural threads that pull against appreciating ourselves. Somehow, it's seen as self-congratulatory, not humble, or plain egotistical. We beg to differ. It's a vital, essential key to achieving Brilliant Health.

This next story is one of our favorites, about how we personally witnessed a very dramatic example of the curative powers of Appreciation.

THE CURE

Several years ago we sat in a room with twenty-five students taking part in their first day of an intensive, yearlong master's degree program in accounting. We watched the increasingly stressed-out students as a faculty panel addressed them. "If you want to succeed in this program," the professors told the rapt young people, "you'll have to give up your entire life for the next twelve months." The professors left the room, and the students sat in stunned silence. Each one looked like the proverbial deer caught in the headlights of an oncoming truck. We were up next.

Fortunately, the students got over their shell shock, and things improved as we set about introducing exercises on each of the nine Brilliant Health practices. By midafternoon, as we worked through an Appreciation exercise, we walked among the small groups, hearing students shower one another with first-day Appreciations: "I appreciate your thoughtful questions." "I appreciate your glowing smile." "I appreciate your funny stories at lunch." At the end of the day one of the students, Kelly, approached us in tears. To our relief, her tears weren't anxious ones—they were joyful.

Kelly explained that, since childhood, stressful situations had always triggered debilitating stomach cramps that left her bedridden. No doctor had been able to diagnose the cause, and once these horrible pains began to set in, no medical intervention or medication had helped. To make matters worse, Kelly was stressed not only by events everyone else might consider difficult, but in anticipation of occasions that should be cause for celebration. Chosen to be maid of honor at her sister's wedding, for example, Kelly was forced to miss the ceremony because her stomach pains became too intense. When her college volleyball team went to the state championship, she stayed back in the hotel. The first day of every highly anticipated vacation, something most of us look forward to with enthusiasm, was, for Kelly, another catalyst for her painful symptoms.

Kelly stood with us and shared her story and then extended her arm to each of us, shook hands, dabbed her eyes, and in a shaky voice managed to blubber, "This afternoon, with all the stress, I felt the pain coming on. But miraculously, during the Appreciation exercise, it disappeared. I'm thrilled! I've never been able to stop it before."

When the next episode occurred several weeks later, Kelly ran to the phone and called her mother. "Mom! Quick! Appreciate me!" she pleaded. Her mother's dose of gratitude did the trick: the pain disappeared. Much to Kelly's delight, over the next six months her newfound technique of Appreciation-loading worked wonders.

But it all recurred on the evening that Kelly's boyfriend took her to a romantic dinner and proposed. The excitement, fear, and sheer magnitude of the moment were so overwhelming that she doubled over in pain. She ran back to the phone and dialed her mom for more appreciation. But in spite of her mother's best efforts, the pain persisted.

Appreciation

Kelly's heart sank. Desperate to do anything, she grabbed some paper and madly wrote down everything she appreciated about *herself*. To Kelly's great relief, the pain began to subside. Her brief exposure to desperation led to an immensely important lesson. Ultimately, to get the greatest health benefits from Appreciation, we have to do it for ourselves.

There's a simple yet very profound reason why this works. When others appreciate us, we don't always believe it. We're the only ones who can truly convince ourselves of our own value. While it's unlikely that most of us will have the kind of dramatic success that Kelly experienced, Appreciation is a practice that produces profound physiological changes that can make us healthier.

There's a happy postscript to Kelly' story. She's thriving. Four years later, she has graduated and got through the wedding ceremony without any problems. She's now happily married, has a good job, and continues to successfully manage the ailment with Appreciation whenever she feels the slightest hint of stomach pain.

To enjoy deep self-appreciation, get out a pad of paper and write down all the qualities you most love about yourself (and want others to value in you as well). To help you think about what those might be, we offer some of many examples shared by students in our Brilliant Health workshops: honesty, capacity to love, creativity, ability to inspire other people, inventiveness, fairness, sense of humor, and enthusiasm. Ask a few friends and loved ones to add to your list. You may be pleasantly surprised by what you hear.

WHAT DO YOU MOST VALUE ABOUT YOURSELF?

Sam attended one of our seminars in an effort to better manage his life as a severe diabetic. Somewhat arrogant and aggressive during the session, he was, however, an active participant and worked especially hard attempting to discover what he most valued about himself. But all efforts in that direction proved frustrating. Nothing hit the target.

Three weeks later, when he returned to the follow-up session, his face was different, more open and friendly. His body seemed more relaxed, and his comments to others were more helpful, salient, and heartfelt. When it was his turn to give us an update, he glowed with the satisfaction of a kid who'd just learned to tie his shoes. He'd spent an arduous, self-searching three weeks and finally landed on what he valued most about himself. It was an unlikely conclusion. The thing he valued was what he'd been most ashamed of and vigorously tried to hide for his entire life.

"Ever since I was a small child my family tormented me by saying, 'You're too sensitive! Toughen up. Don't be a wuss.' I hated myself for my sensitivity and covered it over by developing a hard shell. Through the years, I gained a reputation of being uncaring and cold, but it didn't bother me because anything was better than being called a wuss. I always felt weak because I was so sensitive, and now, for the first time in my life, I see it as my power and my strength. I've been denying the real me. I finally got that it's a gift to feel things so deeply."

Sam used Appreciation to overcome messages from his

family. Many of us can use Appreciation to overcome messages from the media.

Appreciating Our Bodies

We spend an inordinate amount of time being bombarded with messages that our bodies are failures. Advertisements constantly tell us we are too short, too tall, too fat, and too hairy. To make matters even more uncomfortable, magazine covers sport already beautifully shaped models further airbrushed into perfection. Product marketing thrives on pointing out imperfections, because nothing ensures sales like a client base looking for salvation from their own perceived physical inadequacies.

Is it any wonder, then, that we find it so difficult to appreciate our own bodies? And what you tell your body to become at a conscious and unconscious level becomes a self-fulfilling command. If your messages from your brain are that you are sick, fat, unhealthy, or ugly, your body will do everything in its physical capacity to comply.

There's no rocket science here. When you believe you deserve good health, you are more likely to act, behave, and think in a way that is best for you. Your body has an incredible desire to be in its healthiest state. The act of self-appreciation is one of the most influential techniques we have to remove some of our negative perceptions. Whether they come from media messages or from childhood experiences, they stand a good chance of being overridden by emotionally positive blasts of self-appreciation.

Expressing Appreciation

As you read this and imagine either being appreciated or expressing appreciation to someone else, it's quite possible you feel uneasy. In our years of guiding individuals through Appreciation exercises, we've noticed that many people have an unexplainable surge of resistance to both expressing and receiving appreciation. In fact, some anticipate the exercise with dread.

We now understand this reaction as a fundamental, biochemically driven emotional hiccup caused by oxytocin, a fascinating neurotransmitter that breaks down the walls around our individual self in order to encourage the building of a new relationship with another person. The intimacy many of us experience after expressing appreciation to others is the result of this complex and sometimes initially uncomfortable chemical chain reaction that first breaks down ego to allow the emotional inclusion of others and then rebuilds it. Without this process, we would have difficulty bonding deeply.

Oxytocin is a rare chemical that is released directly into the bloodstream after being made in the brain. Not only does it have all kinds of wonderful effects on bonding, social interaction, and regulating the stress response, it chemically affects many organs in the body. Though a lot of its functions are unknown, it does beneficially affect blood pressure and other cardiac functions. Thus, expressing appreciation really does feel good to your heart! In our next story, Mesut's mother would agree.

Appreciation

MESUT AND THE EMPTY NEST

On a research trip to the Middle East, we met Mesut (his real name, and one of eight words that translate to *happy* in Turkish). Soon after Mesut moved away from the family home in central Turkey, his mother, Cecil, now childless for the first time in thirty years, began suffering from severe asthma and panic attacks. Her perplexed doctors were unable to come up with a treatment and, by the time her five adult sons had called an emergency confab at their mother's home, the doctors had given up.

"We were shocked at our mother's sudden deterioration," said Mesut, the youngest of the sons. "But, if medicines weren't going to work, we had to make our own attempts to help her."

The sons could only identify one tangible change in their mother's life: the loss of in-person communication with the children who were now scattered all over Turkey. "We pulled up chairs around Mom's bed and, one by one, told her how much we needed and appreciated her. We told family stories and made her understand how important she was in our lives."

Over the next week, the Appreciation sessions continued, and Cecil began to rally. After their initial visit, the sons made calls of appreciation to her in rotation. From Istanbul one son would talk about his earliest pleasant memories; from Ankara, she'd hear about her wonderful cooking. From Ismir, Patara, and Mira, she would be appreciated for sharing her love of books and music with her children.

"The more we talked to her, our mother's asthma subsided and her anxiousness has become almost unrecognizable. She sings on the phone again. She's not the only one who benefits. We feel more connected as a family too."

> Think of someone who would benefit or be thrilled by authentic, deeply felt appreciation from you. Let nothing stop you. Just do it! Pick up the phone, write a letter, send a card, a gift, an email. It really is the "thought" that counts!

When we appreciate someone, we often long to give a gift to that person. Appreciation is, in itself, a wonderful form of giving, both to another and to ourselves. In all cases, giving gifts communicates how much you appreciate and value the receiver.

When a person doesn't have gratitude, something is missing in his or her humanity. A person can almost be defined by his or her attitude toward gratitude.

—ELIE WIESEL (1928–),
Holocaust survivor and
Nobel Peace Prize winner

EIGHT

Giving

That's what I consider true generosity. You give your all, and yet you always feel as if it costs you nothing.

—SIMONE DE BEAUVOIR (1908–1986)

When Ralph Waldo Emerson said, "No man can sincerely help another without giving to himself," he couldn't possibly have known the medical and scientific accuracy of his statement. In fact, 121 years after his death at a ripe old age, longevity researchers at the University of Michigan would prove just how important giving is. They found that older people who did *not* give practical or emotional support to others—helping with transportation, shopping, housework, errands, or child care—were more than twice as likely to die over a five year period as people who consistently helped spouses, friends, relatives, and neighbors. Even though none of the 423 couples in the study had yet been born, Mr. Emerson might have guessed but could not have so eloquently proved that one of Giving's greatest rewards is the possibility of a longer life and the certainty of a better one.

The eighth Brilliant Health practice is Giving: giving to others, and giving the gift of allowing others to give to us.

How is it that something so basic has such a radical impact on health? New research shows that giving truly does have far-reaching effects on the brain and body. In a study of patients with severe rheumatoid arthritis, those who underwent training to become volunteers helping others with the disease had significant reductions in pain, improved cognitive scores, and improved mood. One even claimed, "It's almost as if I've stopped aging and started to get younger!"

Just thinking about giving seems to be beneficial. Studies done at the University of Wisconsin found that people engaged in compassionate meditation (thinking about compassion and giving) created greater activity in the parts of the brain linked to happiness, rational thought, and creativity.

Think about the times you've given and the times you've been given to. How does it feel? If you had other giving opportunities, whom could most benefit from receiving your gifts, and what would those gifts be?

In the next story you'll see just how exceptionally potent giving can be in the creation of positive emotions.

BONNIE'S LONGEVITY PUZZLE

Bonnie has joined a very select club: the rare group of patients who've lived more than three years past a diagnosis of pancreatic cancer. This type of survivorship is a complex phenomenon caused by factors that are not easily discerned. Yet we share Bonnie's story because she credits Giving as a major piece of her longevity puzzle.

Bonnie had lived in the United States for all of her life until leaving for a new home in Thailand with her husband in 2001. For the first two years she enthusiastically immersed herself in learning about the local culture. On a short trip back to the States she saw her doctor for a routine visit, mentioning a few episodes of stomach pain. After extensive testing she was given the devastating diagnosis of pancreatic cancer, a disease for which the survival time is generally less than one year. Assuming she had little time left, Bonnie flew back to Thailand to spend her remaining days with her husband.

"I had begun to feel terrible burning pain in my abdomen even before I got back to Thailand. But shortly after my return, when I was invited to spend a few days volunteering with a local orphanage, something bizarre happened. When I was with the children, I didn't feel the pain. So I offered to come every day. It's the only time my world seemed right. The love and calmness I felt gave me a sense of security, and I could forget about the loneliness and fear for those few hours each day."

Greg got the chance to accompany Bonnie on one of her daily visits to the orphanage. When she arrived, the children came running. The energy exchange was unmistakable, her eyes shone brightly, and the love bestowed on her was overwhelming.

Bonnie continues to receive treatments from Asian doctors in Thailand and Western-style treatments from her amazed doctors in the United States. And she still makes daily visits to the orphanage. It would be impossible for any of us to know what factors most influence her wellness—genetics, diet, acupuncture, or Western medicine—but she credits her work with the orphans as being "the most curative treatment of all." By taking advantage of all the healthy choices she could make, along with the best of current medicine, she fought all the odds and climbed upward on the staircase of Brilliant Health.

Bonnie's experience is consistent with large studies of givers, who often experience two separate stages in the practice of Giving. Though those stages are incompletely understood by modern medicine, the first is often described as a rush of good feeling that is likely created by an immediate, powerful dose of endorphins and adrenaline. The second stage is a sense of calm. This calm is a culmination of multiple alterations in brain states evoked by true, authentically delivered giving. Giving and its emotional siblings, compassion and empathy, all focus our attention on now. This perspective produces a potpourri of benefits: relieving physical stress, enabling blood flow, deepening our breathing, facilitating digestion, relaxing muscles, and restoring immune function.

ONE CHILD OR A BILLION DOLLARS?

We all know that large philanthropic bequests generate a lot of attention and, perhaps, get results. From a social standpoint, size matters. From a physical standpoint, all giving, regardless of the gift's size, has health payoffs. In fact, researchers have found that Bonnie's form of direct aid has distinct advantages. When our giving involves personal contact and connection with the people we help, we may reap even greater health gains, such as fewer colds and episodes of flu, quicker recovery from surgery, relief from insomnia, and even a reduced tendency to overeat. Regardless of how we give, it is certain that giving when we feel most emotionally downtrodden or depleted is a great way to increase our energy resources, create connectedness, and, ultimately, to build community.

Creating the Human Community

As a species, we are social creatures who need human interaction to thrive. We feel most energized when we belong to a community, including being part of social organizations, belonging to supportive families, having loving friends, and taking part in intimate relationships, a community of two.

Lack of community has a physical impact. A group's formal shunning of individual members can cause mental breakdown, even death, and institutionalized babies who are not touched might either die or be mentally and physically crippled for life. It's a well-validated fact that many prisoners consider lockup in solitary confinement as a punishment worse than death.

There are two simple things you can do to create your own community: first, give to others, and second, allow others to give to you.

The Marketplace of Giving

Each of us can enhance our sensation of Brilliant Health by being part of what we call the Marketplace of Giving. This marketplace does not have a physical location. Rather, it's any group of people involved in the cycle of giving and receiving. In this marketplace, individuals offer up the best of their skills, material resources, knowledge, emotional support, and even the sweat of their labor. And they receive in return. It works much like historical bazaars, souks, and village barter exchanges. One family's product is another's need, and vice versa. All the essentials of life, including nonmaterial things like mutual aid and support, are traded in a network that binds individuals into one self-supporting and self-protecting community. And if the candle maker, or weaver, or dairy farmer withdraws, the community is weakened until those skills and products can be reintroduced.

There are many material rewards in this marketplace. But more important than the prosperity it engenders, the cycle of giving and getting supports the health of the community as well as each involved individual. In that sense, it's not so different from the thriving ecology of a rain forest or any of Mother Nature's healthiest organic networks.

An entire healthy community infused with the Marketplace of Giving may seem like a fairy tale. But consider the case of Roseto, Pennsylvania.

A MYSTERIOUS SLICE OF MIDDLE AMERICA

In 1955, public health researchers began to be mystified by the mortality records in the small town of Roseto. They eventually published a documented medical study called "The Roseto Effect."

Weighed against the norm of neighboring small-sized communities, Roseto's citizens broke every accepted good health practice. They drank more alcohol, ate more red meat and fatty food, and exercised and dieted less. Yet they suffered 35 to 40 percent fewer heart attacks than did residents of comparable communities, even those nearby that shared the same water source.

Without any physical clues to explain the difference, researchers began looking at nonphysical factors and noticed the special nature of the town's social networks. Roseto was a community that cherished close family ties, high levels of social support, and low levels of social competitiveness, many of these values dating back to its beginnings as an Italian immigrant community. In other words, Roseto was very much like a village with a close-knit Marketplace of Giving. Its community feeling was the only thing that set it apart.

The researchers followed the town over the ensuing years, during which Roseto's unique "mutually supportive social structure" started to deteriorate, and *so did the good health of the town's residents*. Unfortunately, over time, as their Marketplace of Giving began to crumble under the pressures of modern life in the late twentieth century, Roseto's rate of heart attacks rose to the national average.

The fading of small-town America doesn't mean we can't have a Marketplace of Giving. Each of us can take an active role in creating our own marketplace. Just as Roseto was famous for its tradition of multigenerational family meals, where people could cherish a sense of togetherness and love, we can do the same. Here's how one woman took control of her life and did it for herself.

MARGARET'S INTENTIONAL COMMUNITY

We know a woman named Margaret who, given her life circumstances, could easily feel isolated and lonely. She's divorced and lives alone. She has no family members living near her. And yet despite this apparent solitude, Margaret is one of the most widely embraced people we've ever met. We're not simply referring to someone who's collected a wide circle of friends. Though one could certainly describe Margaret's situation in those terms, there's much more to Margaret's community than that.

Margaret's community is so wonderful and inspiring because it is born of her simple Core Intention to give something to every person she meets. She's created a unique Marketplace of Giving in which the things exchanged aren't necessarily expensive or even tangible. Margaret's giving might take the form of a compliment, an offer to help with a chore, or a small, personalized gift tied up in a bow.

More important than *what* Margaret gives is *how* she gives. She has no desire for a return, offering her gifts for the simple reason that doing so engenders inside her a deep and profound satisfaction. In other words, she does it because it feels good. Margaret's always on the search for a newspaper article, a referral, or a phone number that might help someone.

Famous for her dinner parties, Margaret loves to cook, and through these generous and entertaining meals, she's brought together a core group of friends. These meals are a great metaphor for the nurturing and nourishing quality of Margaret's Core Intention. Not only does Margaret's giving provide her with the simple joys of doing something for others, it's also inspired her friends to give back the best they have in return.

What are the goods in Margaret's marketplace? One of them is mutual support during hard times, such as illness, family difficulties, career challenges, and similar troubles. Another common exchange is simply the sharing of resources around financial advice, intellectual growth, cultural experiences, and celebrations. The lucky coparticipants in Margaret's Marketplace of Giving bring their amazing and varied gifts to all the participants, and, in times of need, can count on the unquestioning and nonjudgmental support of those who share in this marketplace.

This highly integrated system of trusted friends is the essence of intentional community. Most of us have experience with accidental communities that arise from arbitrary circumstances like blood relations and organizational groupings such as neighborhoods or schools. In contrast, the essence of intentional communities is that they are groups of people formed by choice. Its members are handpicked by you. Ideally, each person who's part of your community has an intention to support you, just as much as your intention is to support them. You can build your own community by choosing trusted extended family members, groups of friends, fellow church members, and colleagues in the workplace. The only requirement for membership is that everybody offers up the best of themselves, their passions, capabilities, and resources. And, while they give, they also receive from you.

Think about your own Marketplace of Giving. Who are the people in it? Who might you also include? What gifts might you offer?

SUPPORT: THE DOCTOR'S PRESCRIPTION

A key to Brilliant Health is to spend as much time as possible with those whose intention it is to honor and support us. And we can choose to limit the time devoted to those who don't honor and support us, even though they may be intractable fixtures in our lives.

Kevin is director of health services at a community agency in Southern California. "There is no question that the people who do best have a strong support system," he says. "They've got people in their lives who they love and who they let in to support them. The people who tend to do worse isolate themselves when they get sick and actually push away those who want to help."

Statistics on survival after heart attacks, breast cancer, and even recoveries from colds bear this out. However, there are many variations, and thus debate, on what works best as support for patients in illness. Some scholarly articles point to the benefit of structured support group programs after cancer. Other research suggests the support of a single person is most important. And still others conclude that structured counseling with professional therapists is most advantageous.

Despite the many variations, the central truth is clear: adequate social support is linked powerfully to positive health outcomes. Since what works for one doesn't work for all, it's up to you to define the kinds of support you most need in your life.

CHASING AWAY THE BLUES WITHOUT THE GREEN

One of the most enduring and encouraging aspects of the Marketplace of Giving is this somewhat paradoxical truth: although the marketplace does not have to spring from material wealth or abundance, and often does not, it always engenders a special kind of wealth. Think of it as the best investment you'll ever make.

One of our favorite examples of this is Ms. Mabel, a wonderful seventy-five-year-old. We visited her not long ago at her home in the South Central district of Los Angeles. We turned out to be among her last visitors.

Ms. Mabel had not had an easy life. Money had always been scarce. She had had her share of health challenges. In her childhood she was diagnosed with juvenile diabetes. She had also had her share of tragedy. During one horrific week ten years previously, her adult son was killed in a hit-and-run accident, and then, five days later, her house and all her worldly goods burned to the ground.

It might be hard to imagine that a person who has had such a rough time of it could be so generous with giving, and yet that's exactly how Ms. Mabel has lived her life. Despite all the setbacks thrown at her, she has always been focused on what she can give to those around her. "Giving to others has been my medicine," she says of her approach. "It's given me the energy and joy to live the most wonderful life. My motto is this: 'Don't look for good where you give it.' When you're not searching for something in return and give freely from your heart, then you find real joy."

So what, exactly, could a person like Ms. Mabel have to

give? Like many of those who enthusiastically participate in the Marketplace of Giving, Ms. Mabel had always been aware of her talents and knew how to bring them to the service of others. In her case, she was a talented cook, so she always came up with creative and inexpensive ways to cook for all the neighborhood kids who didn't have a meal. She once baked one hundred sweet potato pies for a school fund-raiser.

She also gave of her gifts as a mother. Although part of her income came from raising several foster children, it was not just a way for her to make a living but a vocation she embraced in the fullest, most loving spirit of giving. Even after her foster children were grown and living on their own, she continued to be a mother to them. And every kid in Ms. Mabel's neighborhood knew they could share their troubles with her, get some sage advice, and count on her to offer a safe haven in an otherwise dangerous world.

As she reflected on her life, she remembered how, in the 1960s, she had uprooted her husband and four children and decided to leave the Baptist community where they lived in Mississippi and venture across the country, to enjoy California's culture of openness and abundance. She wanted to give her kids a sense that it was a good thing to revel in the simple joy of a beautiful day, to exult in one's good health, to have prosperity, and, most important, to not feel guilty about it.

Ms. Mabel maintained her lifelong participation in the Marketplace of Giving and, in her own way, it truly was the best investment she ever made. Despite her life with diabetes and her misfortunes, her "medicine" of giving helped her thrive. For example, she maintained her eyesight twenty years longer than her doctors expected, and she lived far beyond medical predictions. In the closing days of her life she told a story not of hardship and poor health but one of joy. By nourishing others literally, with lovingly prepared food, and figuratively, with her deep reserves of maternal strength, she was sustaining herself on an abundance of love that had been returned to her. She intentionally created long-term emotional connections with hundreds of people, and those connections brought her a life of genuine richness.

Giving Back

One of the most positive healing choices we've seen repeatedly in our journeys is when people turn their illness or disability into an opportunity to help others.

Here's how some of them do it:

- When Tom developed the misunderstood neurological condition called dystonia, noted for its sustained muscle contractions and odd repetitive movements, he exhausted every medical avenue until he finally found relief in the traditional Chinese practice of qigong. He's spent the last four years posting his findings on the Internet and volunteering to talk to anyone else who suffers from the disease.

- After an unanticipated colon cancer surgery, Linda initially told her family not to utter a word about it to anyone. Over time, her emotional freedom came from speaking at corporate "lunch-n-learn" programs about the importance of colonoscopies in cancer prevention.

• One year after Andy's kidney transplant, he looked for a way to make his life meaningful and inspirational to others. After pushing himself to bike ride across the United States, he made it his passion to provide hope to patients waiting for an organ match by speaking about his expedition.

There are many people in our world who give richly. But let's also note that our society has some weird and ambiguous notions about the nature of giving. We want to specify what thoughtful, productive, brilliantly healthy giving is *not*.

From Martyr to Manipulator: When Giving Goes Bad

Giving isn't a wholesale behavior. The twelfth-century philosopher, Maimonides, zeroed in on the least exalted type of charity, and coined it "morose giving." Morose giving happens when we don't really want to give. It's feeling forced by our boss to write the check to charity or attending a benefit event when we'd rather not. It's begrudgingly baking a casserole for a neighbor. And, if we descend into moroseness, remember that, just when our check is cashed or someone takes the first bite of casserole, we've put ourselves in a negative and self-destructive biochemical state that ultimately hurts us and the community.

There are a good number of socially acceptable yet miserable giving styles that would not pass Maimonides' scrutiny. In fact, he wouldn't certify them as giving. To him these would be *non-giving*. Even though these days it's bandied about in glowing terms, the most common form of nongiving is *sacrificing*, that is, depleting ourselves in favor of another person, family, or career and feeling bitter about it. When we sacrifice, we're leaving behind a terrible guilt load while we rob ourselves and, perhaps our families, of needed resources. Another news maker is *martyrdom*, in which we harm ourselves for a belief or cause, leaving us painfully burning at the stake while our adversaries enjoy their enemy's diminished ranks. *Controlling others by giving* to them is manipulation of the highest order, a sleight of hand that may initially look like generosity but fools no one, particularly when you do it only to get something in return. *Serving others* without asking, "Am I serving them well?" could actually be a *dis*service. And *giving unnecessary gifts* to appear generous simply weighs down the recipient. All these forms of giving are erosive, and none will leave us in a healthy state.

Allowing Others the Dignity to Give

Giving offers yet another service to members of the Marketplace: the gift of allowing others to give back to us. When we do so, it confers value on them and affirms the meaning and importance of what they bring to our lives. It's a wonderful way to let people know they're worthwhile and respected.

Yet, sometimes we stop others from giving to us when we inadvertently interrupt the giving cycle with humble-sounding and self-negating phrases like "Don't be silly, it was nothing," or "I'm fine, I don't need anything." The best answer when somebody wants to give you something is "Thank you so much."

> How do you allow other people to give to you? In what ways do you welcome them and honor them for helping you?

THE PROFESSIONAL HELPER NEEDS HELP

As executive director of a nonprofit organization helping people find affordable housing, Cesar was a professional giver. He was also a personal giver. Cesar donated money, time, and energy unsparingly, and consulted for free with other organizations. Then, at age forty-nine, he was diagnosed with multiple sclerosis. But, like so many of the people we met during research for this book, as his physical health deteriorated, his giving grew.

Cesar's disease progressed to the point where he'd fall down in the street. At first, when Good Samaritans tried to assist, he'd gently push them away. "I was worried about what they'd think of me, but deep down I was actually mortified and scared at the thought of not being able to help myself. I'd never learned how to be vulnerable and ask for help."

But there came a day when Cesar lost so much muscle control that he had no choice but to become a receiver.

"I never expected to have one of my biggest insights lying facedown on the street, but that's what happened. I took a hard fall and saw how tenderly a bunch of strangers rallied to my rescue. I felt their humanity and compassion and willingness to get me up, and could see how a random group would unhesitatingly form into a good-natured pickup team. They really felt good about themselves. From that day on, I welcomed anyone who came to my aid. And when they did, I got a jolt of energy from it."

Cesar initiated a new phase in his previously one-sided giving. By learning to be open to receiving, he created new neural pathways and thus changes in his own biochemical environment. What's more, his willingness to receive elevated the emotions of everyone in the spontaneous community that came to his aid.

Global Community

When we break the giving cycle, we're eroding the reciprocal bonds that hold entire communities together, even globally. With the intention of giving, but forgetting the receiving, the Marketplace of Giving has tragically and frequently gone awry on a grand scale. Think about an international aid worker traveling to a remote part of the world to give the gift of technology or literacy. If the aid worker's attitude is that he's conferring something of great value on the locals, who have nothing of value to give him in return, he is fundamentally disaffirming the very people whom he aspires to help. This form of one-way giving, paternalism if you will, generates hostility rather than gratitude and has been equally disastrous for American aid organizations, religious missionaries of all types, and the white-suited cultural attachés of the old British Empire.

On the other hand, if our aid worker thinks indigenous cultures have beliefs and practices of beauty and worth, and he receives them with an open heart, there's a far greater chance that his gifts will be happily embraced by people whose value he has acknowledged.

Giving on any scale—personal, community, worldwide—generates beautiful, intimate partnerships and meaningful alliances, associations, and unions. All of these are good for our health. But in order for us to get the benefits of these connections, our giving must be honest and truly come from the heart.

The act of nutrition is not a purely physiological event . . . The family meal is a formality that cultivates in us . . . a capacity for sharing, generosity, thoughtfulness, a talent for civilized conversation.

—FRANCINE DU PLESSIX GRAY (1930–)

NINE

Truth

All truths are easy to understand once they are discovered;
the point is to discover them.

—GALILEO GALILEI (1564–1642)

We all know dishonesty erodes interpersonal relationships, organizations, and our society, but fewer of us know how brutal it is on our bodies. In fact, Truth is the Brilliant Health practice that scientists can most clearly and unquestionably connect to our immediate physical well-being. It's well-documented that when we lie, our blood pressure rises, respiration grows shallow and more rapid, pulse rates zoom, and we perspire.

When John Larson developed the first polygraph in 1921, these were among the symptoms it measured to detect when a person was lying. More recent inventions also identify that when we tell lies, our skin temperature rises by as much as nine degrees Celsius, and there are stress-related trembles in our voices.

This isn't late-breaking news, though. In ancient China, criminal suspects were tried with a doctor in attendance who watched for changes in heartbeat and skin temperature to certify the veracity of their testimony. Four thousand years later, scientists are discovering that lying activates areas in the brain associated with stress responses. This elevation of tension, anxiety, and physical illness resulting from untruth makes perfect evolutionary sense: we're physically punished for lying because it disrupts the essential relationships and networks that both protect us and make us successful as a species. So, over time, telling untruths is the personal and social equivalent of being hit by a Mack truck. Positive emotions give us the smooth ride of a Rolls-Royce and are the reward we get for speaking the truth.

The final Brilliant Health practice is Truth: telling ourselves the truth and eliminating the lies we tell others. Given the serious physiological effects of lying, Brilliant Health requires that we have a personal contract to tell the truth to our loved ones, our caregivers, our friends and colleagues, and, most important, to ourselves. For the sake of our own survival and well-being, it's apparent why the natural default position of our human brains is set on *truth*.

What Is Truth?

Wouldn't it be great if there were a simple answer to this question? If you've struggled with your own special definition for the word truth, you're not alone. It's been the subject of centuries-long debates: from philosophy to marketing, science to spirituality, personal psychology to social dynamics, disagreements rage on about the topic. Our intention is not to fuel them but to pinpoint what Truth means when seen through the lens of Brilliant Health.

So, after consolidating all of our research, here's the truth about truth. In relation to health, it has two widely used meanings. The first is the practical one we call *Factual Truth*, which is observable. Either I am, or I am not, sitting in a wheelchair. Only the most far-out philosopher would argue with this factual truth.

The second category is trickier and more nuanced. This form of truth is our authentic viewpoint or interpretation of a situation. We call it *My Truth*. For example, consider the statement, "Even though I'm sitting in a wheelchair, I'm a healthy person." The "I'm a healthy person" part of the remark is open to interpretation. If a doctor heard it, she might disagree on the basis of medicine. However, if I made the statement out of a belief I honestly hold about my overall quality of life with no intention of misleading myself or others, then it's My Truth.

From the standpoint of Brilliant Health, our bodies are equally rewarded by both types of truth. And you get that reward whether a doctor, or anyone else for that matter, believes it's true. But there's one warning: when it comes to My Truth, you're not rewarded if your truth comes in the form of an unaccountable self-deprecating assessment or a verbal attack on others.

Factual Truth

THE POWER OF TRUTH

Most of us have heard the old saying, "The truth shall set you free." It sounds simple enough, but confronting the truth, in all of its forms, can often be one of life's greatest challenges. Much of the difficulty comes not so much from facing the truth but from *knowing* what truth is. Even when we decide to face the truth, we can find ourselves lost, wandering far from the places where it lives. And, to be sure, there are simpler basic truths about the world around us that we might allow to become obscure for many reasons, such as when we avoid certain subjects because we're afraid of them or retreat into fantasy because reality is too hard to bear. The reasons are myriad, but the result is the same: we allow ourselves to live in the fog of self-deception.

The first step of planting our feet firmly in reality is to confront the simple facts of our lives. Many of these facts are basic. Without an acknowledgment of the factual truths of our lives, we can't set the most helpful intentions or take action to change.

ALWAYS MOVING TOWARD TRUTH

Before you continue, we'd like to make another point about truth: There isn't one ideal time for recognizing it. As we talked with medical professionals, we became aware of readiness factors. All of us have to approach the truth on our own timetable. Sometimes it is absolutely apparent up front. Other times, the truth unrolls as we explore. And sometimes we need to use denial, that is, avoidance, as protection against the suddenness of a trauma. Some truths are too big to digest all at once, like the death of a loved one, a shocking diagnosis, or a sudden physical trauma. But the main impulse in Brilliant Health is that you are always moving toward the truth.

THE MIRROR IMAGE

Imagine waking up in the morning knowing that your face might have become grotesquely scarred during the night. Would you run to the mirror? Would you lie in bed to delay confronting the truth of your new face?

We delved into this topic during a fascinating discussion with Elizabeth, the leader of a facial reconstruction surgical unit for cancer patients in the Southwest. These procedures have the most visible results of any type of surgery, The outcomes range from modestly altered facial features to radical—even disfiguring—changes. These operations certainly save lives, but the patients' physical identities are often forever changed.

"Even though everyone has a different readiness factor," Elizabeth told us, "some patients want to see the surgical results quickly. Others avoid the facts for a very long time. Those who most want to look in a mirror see the reality quickly and begin to come to terms with their new physical appearance, usually with a large dose of acceptance and appreciation for the fact that their lives may have been saved. These are the patients who heal the fastest. The longer patients avoid the truth, the longer it takes them to integrate back into their families and communities. Patients who can't bear to look at themselves and see the truth about how they will now appear to others seem to take much longer to recover."

Sometimes factual truth is visible only to ourselves, but, as Jeff learned, coming to terms with the truth is a step toward health.

REFLECTIONS ON THE TRUTH

The story of Jeff is a good illustration of how we are sometimes forced to confront the truth, and how we can make active choices to deal with the facts we're dealt. Jeff, a forty-five-year-old cabinetmaker, went in for a medical checkup not long ago, and as part of his physical, he received a blood screening that included an HIV antibody test.

When his HIV test came back positive, it was an emotional shock. But despite the life-altering nature of the news, Jeff didn't wait long to begin preparing himself for the critical choices he'd have to make. "I didn't seek out the facts earlier, or I might not have been in that position," he says of his previous state of denial about HIV. "Now that I was HIV positive, though, having good information was crucial for protecting my own health and that of others, so I made sure I had a lot of information."

He began to research HIV. If he'd made the mistake of not knowing enough before he received the news of his positive status, he decided that he would change as a result of his new awareness.

Now Jeff has a personal contract with himself to tell the factual truth. "Frankly, I don't have time to lie, whether to others or to myself. Telling the truth is easier. It burns less of my energy, and it requires much less time management than lying. It's healthy, and it's my personal path of least resistance."

Clearly, Jeff reached this point with the intent to be truthful, but he has a host of other intentions. These include following medical instructions, staying medically informed, and not doing anything that would jeopardize the health of others. All of these intentions are outgrowths of Jeff's recognition of the factual truth. "As to my immediate future, my intentions are all based on truth, so I have a fantastic, well-informed road map of how I'll take action," he says.

Jeff's story provides a powerful illustration of the interaction between truth and intentions. In fact, it suggests an important truth-telling scenario we can follow up the staircase to Brilliant Health:

- First, if we have the facts, that is, the truth, we will set our most effective truth-informed Intentions.

- Second, because we have set clear Intentions grounded in the bright light of reality, we have an open, unobstructed view of the path on which our Intentions need to take us.

Confronting the factual truth allowed Jeff to get the ball rolling. But it's extremely important to understand what's at stake and what can happen if we don't embrace our reality. If Jeff hadn't searched for the truth, he would never have been able to set meaningful, productive Intentions. If his intentions had been uninformed, there would have been no way he could have taken appropriate and accountable actions. Truth is the guide for all positive, life-affirming behavior. We need it as a compass. Without it, we're lost in the wilderness.

None of the Brilliantly Healthy people we interviewed were in denial about any of their illnesses. In fact, they were all well-informed about their bodies. They were also straightforward about their health issues, and they had a thorough understanding of the matrix of environmental, behavioral, and genetic factors that come together to create their own unique state of health.

State a Factual Truth about your health. Be sure it isn't a judgment, interpretation, emotion, or demand. Having stated the truth, how do you feel?

Factual Truth is the unambiguous kind of truth. Personal truths are an entirely different animal: interpretive, equivocal, and malleable. But, they're ours. No one can take them away from us.

My Truth

There is only one way to judge the truth of a personal truth, and it's in the form of a question: Do you tend to mislead yourself or others? If you intend to fool others or outfox your own body, you are not telling a personal truth. But if you believe your own statements and intend to mislead no one, particularly yourself, you are speaking your personal truth.

MY TRUTH, THE SHOULDS, AND YOUR HEALTH

My Truth may run in opposition to all the social directions and demands we receive from the media, our loved ones, our churches, and our jobs. These shoulds are other people's truths, but they may not be right for us. If you drop the shoulds that are not in alignment with your own personal truths, you save yourself from the negative physical effects of untruth. In fact, you will have the Brilliantly Healthy sensation of clarity, independence, and well-being that comes from telling the truth.

> State your Truth about your health. How do you interpret or judge your state of wellness or a health issue you're dealing with now? Is your statement from your heart and free of the judgments and needs of others? Can you live comfortably with your truth?

THE PICTURE OF DORIAN GRAY

In Oscar Wilde's *The Picture of Dorian Gray*, a handsome, eternally youthful man lives a corrupt and depraved life while his portrait in the attic ages grotesquely. The hidden portrait records the physical truth of his dissolute, violent, and dishonest self.

The horror of Dorian Gray's portrait represents the great hurrah for truth. When it comes to Brilliant Health, no matter how we hide the facts, stop listening to our bodies, avoid reality, kid ourselves, or scream and shout to the heavens, the truth will emerge and, as we'll see in Max's story, the body is one canvas on which it will certainly be expressed.

MAX'S BODY

Max had always been a con artist. As a young man growing up in New York City in the late 1940s, hustling was not only his means of survival, it became his way of life. By the 1950s, Max knew a lot of the right people, and he parlayed those connections into an entry-level job at a public relations firm. Technically, Max was nothing more than a gofer, driving clients to and from important engagements and taking care of other less-than-glamorous duties. But, hustler to the core, Max used his manipulative skills to con his employer's world-famous clientele into believing that he was a high-rolling publicist.

He hosted dinners at the Copacabana and other swanky nightspots. He rented a pricey penthouse on the East Side. But propping up his fantasy life was expensive, to say the least, and well beyond Max's means. He was, in fact, facing bankruptcy, and it wasn't long before his boss uncovered Max's grand deceptions.

After his life imploded in New York, Max decamped to the West Coast, landing in Los Angeles in the early 1960s, just in time to put his lies to work once more and cash in on the California rock-and-roll scene. Soon he was managing and producing some of the biggest names in the business, and by conventional standards, he was a huge success. He had even married a woman, Danielle, whom he referred to as "the love of my life." They had a child and a new home in Beverly Hills. But although Max's street smarts, smooth talking, and manipulations appeared to have taken him far, he was really going nowhere, and his body was paying the price.

"This life was killing me," says Max, recalling his dawning awareness of how it all began to catch up with him. "My chest felt like it was going to explode. All my senses were dulled. I was a thirty-year-old in the body of an old man. I was also doing more drugs than seems possible and having sex with every woman I could get my hands on, even in groups of two or three. Still, my wife, Danielle, thought I was faithful. I was living a double life."

Max became convinced that the stress of this double life was wreaking havoc on his system, and he believed the only way out was to end his marriage with Danielle. On Christmas Day, 1968, Max drove to the house he shared with Danielle to tell her he couldn't be married to her anymore. Tormented by the guilt of betraying the one person he really loved, he decided that it was better to push her away in one quick, violent discussion than to continue lying to her.

"I expected Danielle to throw a lamp at me and kick me out," he says, "but she didn't. She said, 'Just answer me truthfully one time: have you been faithful to me?' What did I have to lose? I said, 'No.' Then she said, 'Have you been unfaithful more than once?' I said, 'You promised to ask only *one* question,' and I started to feel sick. But I answered her, 'Many times.' She asked more questions. And suddenly we were on a roll. I couldn't stop telling her the truth."

Max's confession turned into what he calls "an orgy of truth-telling" that lasted for forty-eight hours. There were flashes of terror, laughter, crying, and shouting. Max revealed to Danielle everything about his life: the lies, the cheating, and the drug use. Once they got past the factual lies, he shared his interpretations, feelings, and thoughts about what had been driving him. And he listened, deeply, to Danielle's truth. The result was not just psychological relief. Amazingly, there was a stunning physical transformation as well.

"I can't explain it," says Max about the aftermath of his truth-telling. "All my senses went into overdrive. My eyesight got so sharp, every twitch, wrinkle, and gesture was in fine focus. My hearing registered even the sound of Danielle's breathing. All told, the sensory overload made my head feel as if it would fly off. 'Enough stimulation!' I thought. I ran to the toilet and flushed a full ounce of cocaine down it. I lit a cigarette, but I couldn't even inhale. I haven't smoked since. In my entire life, I have never felt so connected to another person as I did to Danielle in those two days of truth-telling. To make things even weirder, an image of a book I read in high school, *Siddhartha*, kept appearing in my mind."

It's not surprising that Herman Hesse's famous novel should spring into Max's mind. It's a story about deep, spiritual enlightenment, and after many years of denial and the numbness of continued deception, Max had become mindful. In doing so, he had activated neural pathways that awakened his senses, changed his biochemistry, and released energy that had long been buried.

In the immediate aftermath of his cathartic truth-telling, and for many years after, Max's senses and physical appearance were altered. "I was carrying myself differently, not hunched over," he says. "Suddenly I was four inches taller, and I am *still* four inches taller. I had some kind of new appearance, and my face must have changed, because people I knew well passed me in the streets and didn't recognize me. I was so tuned in, I felt as though I was experiencing everything as if it was happening for the first time."

Like the title character in *The Picture of Dorian Gray*, Max had long covered his deceptive core with all the trappings of outward success. By embracing the truth, Max allowed himself to reverse that process and to heal. Truth changed Max's portrait of himself for the better.

"Truth is everything," Max says today. "And it can be so easy. It's like trying to find a light switch in the dark. You search and you search and maybe it takes a long time, but once it's found, all you do is flick the switch. Tell the truth to yourself and others, and your life becomes good."

JUST WHAT THE DOCTOR ORDERED

Max's experience dovetails with one of the most interesting statements about truth made during our research interviews. An MD who's also a doctor of Oriental medicine told us:

"Our bodies are like a family system. Just as lying hurts the entire family, lying to ourselves sends the wrong message to our bodies and negatively affects our immune systems. When we tell our bodies a lie like, 'I'm not really sick or tired,' it sends an untrue and confusing message. Unrealistically optimistic people are the same as unrealistic pessimists. They are giving their body an untrue message and are not communicating about how it really needs to respond.

"Whatever you tell your body, it will do its best to make it come true. But don't confuse your body. It will respond with an unconfused physical reality, usually in the form of sickness.

As I tell patients: be careful, get ahead of the curve, and tell the truth to yourself."

Truth Around the World

Whether we're talking with doctors of Oriental medicine in Vietnam, Western practitioners in the United States, or lay people in Australia, the people we've met in our travels have taught us that the healing power of truth is valued everywhere. Though many other cultural belief systems vary worldwide, the compelling need to tell My Truth is a universal desire of the human family.

While on a trip to South Africa, we met Vuyiseka, a Xhosa community health organizer. "Our tribe tells us you must tell the truth to everyone: your parents, your children, your friends. We may want to hide disease, but you cannot heal unless you tell the truth. And there's no way to tell the truth to others unless you tell the truth to yourself. When you tell yourself the truth, you come out of your dark room and do what's good for you. Telling the truth and expressing your real feelings is good medicine. It creates good self-esteem. Then we all benefit from one person's health."

The health of humans from every culture, race, tribe, and ethnicity profoundly benefits from truth. Thus, the need to tell the truth is one of our universal human traits. It is also a critically important element in the creation of vigorous interpersonal relationships and entire communities. And it is the last but certainly not the least of the essential practices of Brilliant Health.

Truth is the only safe ground to stand upon.

—ELIZABETH CADY STANTON (1815–1902)

PART THREE

Transformation

Research into Brilliant Health revolutionized our thinking about the nine practices. In fact, it turned our assumptions upside down. We had assumed that the field of health would mirror the world of happiness, that optimal health would be the outcome of using all of the behaviors in the model concurrently. We were wrong. The more we talked to patients and doctors, the more we realized that any one of the practices would have a healing effect. Each is a biochemical powerhouse on its own.

But imagine your incredible feelings of wellness and happiness if you did, in fact, invoke *all* of the Brilliant Health practices. What would your life be like? It would be an extraordinary and ongoing experience of daily delights. You'd set life-affirming *Intentions* by continually choosing your best attitude and behavior. You'd be *Accountable* to these Intentions and wouldn't be trapped in the murk of blame and victim-hood. Envisioning, the use of imagery, and storytelling, all parts of the practice of *Identification*, would animate your life. And *Centralizing* your passions daily would bring you a deep sense of excitement and fulfillment. *Recasting* provides the emotional adeptness to move through life's darkest and most difficult experiences, and opening *Options* would deliver the biochemical highs that come with flexibility, newness, and hope. You would nurture a deep *Appreciation* of yourself and the world around you, and you'd be a full participant in the Marketplace of *Giving*. And you'd revel in telling the *Truth* to yourself and to others. The outcome of all this would be feelings of emotional aliveness and alignment with others around you. You'd be an active participant in your own healthfulness, and would feel capable of dealing with life's challenges, of living with boldness, integrity, and creativity.

In the following chapters we share stories that illuminate Brilliant Health in different life circumstances: living through illness, living into a ripe old age, and living well at the end of life.

TEN

Living Through Illness in Brilliant Health

ERICA'S STORY

In a small apartment overlooking the Hong Kong harbor, a woman in her mid-fifties approaches the window and stands watching the late light of the evening over the water. She's tired. It's been a long day. She's spent most of it at the hospital, talking with patients suffering from serious illness. She has helped them look at their lives and find hope, and she knows how hard the journey can be.

It's on days like this that she likes to stand here and look at the water. It reminds her of the place she came from, half a world away, at the edge of another ocean, in the midst of a different life. Although she feels the demands of her day, she stands watching this new ocean with a deep, sustaining happiness. How did she get here? This is the story she told us over tea in her apartment.

In December 2003, Erica was a vibrant fifty-year-old living with her husband Troy in one of Maine's most picturesque villages. A community leader, Erica also embraced good health in all of its aspects. She did yoga three times a week, maintained a diet of lean meats and vegetables, and had routine medical checkups. She didn't drink or smoke. And in the summer, she couldn't wait to return to her lakeside home for a vigorous swim. Yet nothing prepared her or her husband for what would happen that year.

Early one morning, Erica was visiting her doctor and was stunned to learn that the results of her second mammogram indicated the presence of an almost certain cancer. She sat for a moment in uncomprehending silence, looking at her doctor, hoping for him to throw some doubt on the diagnosis. "This can't be," she said. "Troy and I are leaving for the Bahamas in three days."

"I'm sorry," said her doctor, "but you'll need to unpack those bags. We need to do a biopsy immediately."

During the car ride home, Erica remembers sitting quietly in deep shock. Then, within hours, she was overcome by a stir of confused emotions that settled into a dark feeling of dread. Was this mortality staring her in the face? She wasn't prepared. How could she possibly deal with this threat? As she desperately tore through her intellectual and emotional skills and tried to conjure anything that would help, she remembered the Brilliant Health program, which she had fortuitously attended.

Intention

The Brilliant Health story begins late on the day of her initial diagnosis. "I started at the beginning with Intention," she says. "My first intention was to take one step at a time. I knew being consumed by anxiety would ruin this day and all other days in the future. I said to myself, 'I've got to enjoy each day, even this one.'"

By the next morning, Erica arrived at a set of ongoing Intentions: "This is my only life, it was being threatened, and I felt compelled to live it to the hilt!" she says. "Rather than feeling different and flawed, my Intention was to do everything I could to feel connected to my immediate family and to the human family. We're all mortal. I didn't want to flip out, so I also intended to be patient and thoughtful in dealing with every aspect of this illness."

And Erica did have to be patient. A week later the biopsy results revealed both good and bad news. Although the diagnosis was an invasive carcinoma, it appeared to be a garden-variety tumor and likely treatable at this early stage. Still, Erica knew she'd have to overcome her feelings of panic and choose the most beneficial response in the face of the uncertainty. "Worry wouldn't help. It could only hurt me both physically and mentally," she recalls.

Accountability

"I never allowed myself to think, 'Why me?' Never. In fact, I said to myself, 'Well, why not *me*?'"

Erica next did something unusual and intriguing. As a top manager in a law firm, she framed her diagnosis as the greatest leadership opportunity of her life. She called upon the skills she had honed so well in her professional life to address what was, without a doubt, the greatest personal challenge she had ever faced. She started where every good leader, from presidents to coaches, begins: "I put together my 'dream team,'" she recalls. "These were the go-to people I knew I could rely on."

She aggressively researched the best doctors, surgeons, and support groups. She solicited the support of dear friends and family members, whose backing might be needed in the upcoming months. With the team in place, she felt in control of her life. And it was this support group that helped her prepare for surgery and manage her recovery.

After surgery, the doctors told Erica that with both chemotherapy and radiation there was a 90 percent chance of the tumor *not* returning.

Once again she took responsibility for creating her best outcome. "I sought out other women who'd had breast cancer and asked for their help. Some of them I'd never met before, but I was always received with eagerness and compassion. People are really wonderful. I asked them questions like, 'What's the most helpful thing you did for yourself?' 'How did you cope?' 'What do I need to look out for?' and 'What can I do to be in the ninety percent group?'"

Hair loss is an almost inevitable result of chemotherapy, and one thing Erica did not want was for people to look at her bald head and think, "Oh, that poor woman!" or "She must be on her last legs!" or even, "Maybe she's part of some religious cult!" So Erica went to her dream team for help, inviting her two most glamorous friends on a shopping expedition for the perfect wig and makeup.

"I really wanted to control my own story and not have other people make assumptions about me," explains Erica. "I wasn't ashamed of the hair loss, but I also didn't want to become the focus of attention. My first wig was cut in a short, curly style. I've been wearing my hair the same way ever since."

Identification and Centrality

In the week leading up to her surgery, Erica updated her Bliss List. "For the next seven days I bombarded myself doing the things I most love," she says. "I swam. I took nature walks and surrounded myself with natural beauty. I went up into the mountains for a day of skiing. Every day I visited with another of my closest friends."

Once the surgery was over and the chemo began, she slowed down. The wrinkled piece of paper that held Erica's Bliss List was her constant companion. She kept flowers in the living room, read romance novels, drank quarts of fresh orange juice, and invited friends to come visit.

Recasting

Erica describes her own Recasting process this way: "As it turned out, I really was able to make an opportunity out of each new part of the cancer situation. During every 3 a.m. freak-out I challenged myself to Recast. I Recast chemotherapy, surgery, doctor's visits, my friends' reactions to the cancer, and my own fears. I had a lot of emotions, but I never fell into depression."

In the end, Erica developed an array of opportunities that came as a result of her illness:

- To build a strong network of women friends.

- To learn about my body, and to test my own capabilities, and to regain my feeling of strength and health.

- To enhance my relationship with my very elderly mother by letting her help me and giving her a sense of purpose.

- To shed a lifetime of fear about disease.

Options

Erica had always been a master of structured thinking, coming quickly to closure, and making hard and fast decisions. With cancer, she knew flexibility would serve her best. Flexibility became her new mantra.

"Medical protocol, particularly around surgery, wasn't going to be flexible," she says. "I did have a few surgical options, like choosing the doctor and anesthesiologist, but, actually, the most flexible part of the entire experience was me. I found out that my attitude is malleable and changeable. After the surgery, I worked to stay intellectually and emotionally open. When I was recovering, I started doing yoga again to keep my body flexible, too."

Appreciation

Erica made good progress, and eventually her treatments came to an end. She'd focused all her efforts on overcoming her illness, and she was winning. Ready to celebrate, she felt a deep sense of appreciation for all the people who had rallied to help her.

Erica decided to host a party for everyone who'd played a role in her adventure. The fifty invitees included meal-makers, Reiki masseuses, CAT-scan technicians, doctors and nurses, makeup artists and wig buyers, and a host of friends and supporters, in addition to her family. As the list grew, so did the depth of her gratitude.

Erica told each one of her network of supporters that she not only wanted to celebrate with them, she wanted to celebrate them personally. "I phoned each one and said, 'This party isn't about me or the end of my radiation treatment. It's about thanking you.' My heart was so full of thanks, and this was my way of expressing it."

Each person at the party received flowers and a personal, handwritten note from Erica, and shared a large cake emblazoned with the words "Thank You Dear Friends." She delivered an emotional speech. But it didn't stop there. She continues to celebrate each day. "The party was an important symbolic gesture," says Erica. "Every day I remind myself how extremely lucky I am to be alive. No problem can overshadow my state of appreciation."

Giving

Before the diagnosis, Erica had amassed twenty-five years of emotional equity by giving to her community. After the diagnosis, the community, which she had worked so hard to support, went into overdrive on her behalf. She was overwhelmed by the gifts of service, support, and information she received.

"At first, being the recipient of other people's help made me feel a little sheepish," Erica confesses. "But, as a longtime depositor in the social capital bank account, it was my time to make a few withdrawals. I was very aware that it was my turn to receive, and I decided to let myself feel special."

"When people asked, 'Is there anything I can do?' I said, 'Yes.' I matched their strengths and passions with my needs." From her most organized friend, Erica asked for help coordinating her meals. Another friend was thrilled to make a color-coded chart of who was bringing what when. Another friend, a gardening fanatic, became the manager of all the bouquets and plants Erica received as gifts. A social worker was given the task of helping out with Erica's mother. And Erica's mother was given the job of reading Sherlock Holmes stories to her.

"I wanted to give her the chance to be my mom again, just like when I was a kid."

"It was amazing how much people liked giving," says Erica, remembering her many friends' generosity. "It was the gift of activity, of feeling they had something valuable to share, that they were worthy and important people in my life. The entire network of givers developed a glow about them. In the midst of my health drama, we were all having a lot of fun."

Truth

Truthfulness was one of Erica's biggest challenges. "In the beginning it was so hard for me to accept the truth, I couldn't even consider telling others about it," she says. "But within the first few days, I realized that there were too many important people who needed to know. And just the act of telling them helped me accept the truth, too. It got a little addictive."

She wrote an email explaining the diagnosis and its consequences and sent it to a long list of people in the community. The response was enlightening for Erica: "It brought out dozens of people who wanted to tell me their own truths and share experiences. It was a fantastic educational process for me. I had nothing to hide and no unfinished business. I felt much less stress. It was a good feeling."

Erica also instructed her doctors to tell her the truth at all times and to answer her questions completely. Throughout her treatments, she was fully informed, knew the facts, and was able to make well-crafted decisions about her medical care and her life as a whole.

ERICA, FOUR YEARS LATER

"Ironically, having cancer has improved my quality of life," says Erica, looking back on her experience. "I didn't have the choice about cancer, but I had a choice about everything else. In hindsight, the Brilliant Health model was always there, particularly at the bleakest times. I used the language a lot. I'd say to my husband, 'Troy, would you help me Recast?,' 'What's my Intention?,' and 'What's there to Appreciate right now?' "

Erica points to Intention as particularly vital to her story. "When I was first diagnosed, my Intention was to do everything I could to die an old woman, and not from breast cancer," she says. "Now, after everything, my Intention is to create the highest possible quality of life and to find purpose." And that she has.

Erica's experience with cancer has propelled her into an entirely new life. After living for twenty-five years in the same home, she jumped across a continent and over the world's largest ocean to establish new, healthy, long-term patterns of living.

Erica's personal life has reached peaks of happiness she'd never thought possible. She has conquered cancer, changed all of her living patterns, embraced new people, and created compelling and healthy relationships with all of the historic friendships from her life in Maine.

Erica's life is good. And, of all her changes, the biggest is her new career as a volunteer for people living with life-threatening illnesses. Far from her law office, this work combines her great interest in health with social service, community building, and helping others become the leaders of their own lives. And she carries with her an abiding passion for Brilliant Health.

Erica's postdiagnosis story shows how these behaviors

function as a single, synergistic healing system. She used them as a practical road map and by doing so generated a feeling of control that helped tame her frightening circumstances, improve her health, and, in the long term, attain a quality of life she never thought she could achieve.

You can use all of these practices in a systematic manner, as Erica did, or choose those most likely to help you in the moment. From the outset, Erica's statistical chances of a long life were good. But the Brilliant Health model can be well-used into extraordinary longevity.

Today, there are more than 55,000 people in the United States over the age of 100. And the experts tell us that by the year 2050 that number could be 834,000. To live in Brilliant Health, we would be wise to follow the life choices made by 101-year-old Lou, who is the subject of the next chapter.

ELEVEN

Living Past One Hundred in Brilliant Health

LOU'S STORY

When you live to be more than one hundred years old, you tend to accumulate your share of stories. At 101, Lou has a lot to choose from. Some of her best stories are illuminating and inspiring simply because they bring alive a place, time, and way of life that most of us have only read about.

One of Lou's favorite stories is of how, at five years old, in 1911, she and her family journeyed across the plains in a wagon from the family home in Pawhuska, Oklahoma, to their new home in the Texas Panhandle. It's the place where Lou grew up, and where, in 1920, when she was fourteen, she got married. Her wedding, and how she announced it to her family, is another favorite story. "My folks knew immediately I'd gotten hitched when they saw me come home in a buggy sitting on my sweetheart's lap," says Lou, recalling the day with a big smile. In short order, two sons arrived. And, then, in 1943, her husband built her the home she still lives in today.

The Texas cow town that Lou and her family rode into in 1911 soon became an oil boomtown and benefited from all the wealth that came with oil. But of course the over-the-top prosperity of the oil years didn't last. In more recent times the town has faded into obscurity. Tumbleweeds blow across the highway and through the dry canyons of the surrounding area. Nowadays, there are many more oil wells and cattle than there are people.

But while the town may well be past its glory days, its oldest citizen is thriving. It's been a good life. At a recent family party celebrating her 101st birthday, Lou sported a wide-brimmed hat in magenta (her favorite color), a huge diamond ring, purple fingernail polish, and a glittering magenta dress. Last year, she began taking medication for the first time: ibuprofen, recommended by her sister as "something that might be good for you." Other than some loss of eyesight and hearing, Lou is in great health and is intellectually and physically thriving. She is surrounded by friends from all over the community, and by many generations of family, including her "baby sister," eighty-eight-year-old Sara.

We wanted to know more about Lou, so we also quizzed her granddaughter, affectionately known as Bee.

Intention

The overriding intention that has directed her life is to live happily. "I've always believed that what goes around comes around. That's why I have rules for myself to always be kind and never hurtful," says Lou. "If you're mean to your kids, you'll end up with kids who are mean. I choose to be positive because life is to be enjoyed. I've got grandchildren, great-grandchildren, and one great-great-grandchild, and I believe it's my job to show them how to live a good life by how I behave. At my age, I'm thrilled to live for another day, but you know, I've always been this way."

Accountability

"In this town, gossip is what people do. Everybody knows everybody," says Lou. "My bridge club ladies always talked about people, but I never did. It pulls me down." Her granddaughter, Bee, says, "In spite of the many deaths and downturns she's experienced, including the dustbowl years, she's never expressed a single word of blame. She just doesn't do it." Lou explains her approach with admirable simplicity. "I've chosen it all. I'm not an underdog, or a sufferer, or a fool."

Of course Lou isn't without some regrets. In one of the sadder moments of her life, and against her own better judgment, Lou was convinced by family members to leave her sister's deathbed even though she believed that no one should die without someone there. When her sister did, in fact, pass away alone, Lou avoided any impulse to blame the family and simply said, "If I could do it over again, I would have stayed."

Identification and Centrality

We've combined Identification and Centrality because Lou has a long Bliss List, and, to this day, she does everything on it. "I only do what I love to do," she says, and it's not long before she rattles off, with increasing speed, a litany of specifics: "I love every single person in my family. I love traveling in the front seat of a car. I love baking pies, but I leave the cakes to my sister. I love magenta, and I love meeting new people, and it's a great joy when they come visit me. Actually," she paused, "I really do enjoy a nip of Bailey's in my coffee every morning. I love Mexican food and lemonade, and those margaritas aren't bad. I love the nickel slot machines in Vegas and Reno, and I bring the nickels home with me in bags. When my kids come to visit, I love to play my favorite card game, thirty-one. They all know to bring their own dimes for betting."

Her grandkids consider Lou "inspirational," but they also call her "cutthroat." Apparently, winning is also a big item on her Bliss List. Bee told us, "Grandma will ruin her own hand just to keep someone else from winning." Lou shows up at her granddaughter's home with her little magenta change purse full of dimes and two decks of large-number cards.

But perhaps one of Lou's biggest pleasures is to share her many stories. She glows with enthusiasm when she regales her large family with tales of the early "wagon days," the oil boom, and the Great Depression. Bee and her husband just made a video of Lou's stories, all in one long, two-hour take.

Recasting

At 101, Lou has seen more than her share of deaths. These have included most of her siblings and one of her children, not to mention the deaths of countless friends who have graced her life. Lou is resilient, but she has always needed the benefit of Recasting to help her move through the loss and grief she's experienced.

Lou's most traumatic loss was the death of her son, which happened when she was ninety-one. Until that time, Lou hadn't ever been in a situation where she felt like she couldn't cope. "I never once wondered what she was feeling, because she told us," says Bee, recalling that time. "Grandma was terribly sad. We really worried about her, but then she started to rally. I think she found what was bothering her so much. She told us, 'Kids aren't supposed to go first.' Somehow, understanding the natural order of things helped explain her feelings and helped her cope."

What was the opportunity that Lou found to help come to terms with outliving her own son? It was when she decided to not cover up the loss and try to forget it, but to "fill the void." Most people in their nineties, faced with such a traumatic loss, could be expected to go into a full retreat from life. But not Lou. She pushed herself, in fact, to do exactly the opposite. "Grandma pulled us all in closer and held us tight," says Bee. "Since then, she's engaged with us even more fully and worked harder to support us in whatever we needed. It's her way of healing from the loss."

Options

One of the aspects of Lou's personality that's particularly endearing is her adventurous spirit. And seeing such a quality in someone over one hundred years old is also inspirational. Lou is not closed-minded, or set in her ways as so many seniors are often described. She remains curious about the world around her: about people, about new technology like her new iPod, and about the nightly news. "I love surprises!" says Lou, giving voice to the sense of joy and wonder that animates so much of what she does. "Change excites me, because I need a little variety, now and again. Mind you, I like things my way, but I'm not a creature of habit," she says, admitting to having her share of that's-the-way-things-ought-to-be thoughts. She illustrates her flexibility with a small example: "I like oval serving dishes at dinner. But on my last trip to Dallas to see my granddaughter, she didn't have any oval dishes, so I thought, 'Well, OK, round will do.' "

And Lou is open to change and variety with respect to more than serving dishes. Bee told us that years ago Lou and her late husband gradually stopped going to church because the Sunday routine and church ritual were too monotonous. "She's really spiritual, but she likes to do it in her own way," says Bee.

Appreciation and Giving

Lou is a comfortable and spontaneous giver. One day Bee said to her grandmother, "You don't even have a will. Don't you think you should do one?" Lou's response was, "Honey, if there's anything you want of mine, I'd rather you have it right now." Bee went home with the set of green glassware that she'd sipped lemonade from for the past half century.

"I've been appreciative every day of my life for what this world has given me," says Lou. For close to a century she has been responsible for bringing the pies to all family gatherings. And to this day visitors will always be sent home with their favorite pie along with the feelings of love and comfort they all associate with it.

Lou's impulse to give goes back to her earliest years, and is something she believes is her mother's legacy. She remembers her mother's tremendous generosity in sending out Lou with baskets of food to the hobos along the railroad track. And giving got her into trouble as a child. She talks about the severe reprimand she got for her own naive generosity, because she let a homeless man into the house when her mother wasn't home. By the time her mother got back from town, Lou had cooked a lavish meal for him.

Like many of those who give so generously, Lou does not have much herself. Although her own home is slowly falling into disrepair, she's revered by her family for helping her grandchildren buy their first homes.

For some people, old age can be isolating and depressing. Lou's life could not be more different. She has served as a model of generosity for every generation of her family, and this spirit of giving has become a guiding star of her family's culture.

Truth

"I tell the truth," says Lou. "It's as simple as that." Her grand-daughter confides to us that she's never been in doubt about what Lou is thinking or feeling. As competitive or excited or engaged as Lou may be in the moment, she is absolutely clear about her reactions. "Grandma comes from a generation where everything is hidden. If she'd been typical, we would not know what she was feeling, and we certainly wouldn't have known about her shot of Bailey's in the morning or her gambling," laughs Bee. "Because of that, I've gotten to know her in ways that most people would have never known their grandparent. I can trust her more than just about anyone on this earth, because I can always trust that what she says is what she really thinks. My guess is that's why everyone in town is drawn to her."

Bee says, "My impression of Grandma Lou is that whatever was dealt to her, she made the best of it. I've seen her worry, but only about something specific like my father's illness. When I think of her, I think about someone who's full of high spirits and who has made a life that delights her. I believe I'll live a lot longer if I live just like her."

TWELVE

Living in Brilliant Health at the End of Life

The most compelling question about death may not be "When will I die?" or "How will I die?" but "How *well* will I die?"

Though death and health may seem paradoxical and contrary subjects, as we've interviewed and worked with patients and their caregivers, we've learned how important the Brilliant Health practices can be at the end of life. They can mean the difference between a frightening death overwhelmed by sorrow and anxiety and a dignified and calm experience surrounded by loved ones. While the afterlife may stimulate varied and colorful speculation, our down-to-earth human and very practical predeath needs and hopes are universal to all cultures. Learning how to die in Brilliant Health can give us the comfort of having the means to cope with what is a lifelong fear for many and an inevitability for everyone.

Although our interviews on death and dying have taken place in Africa, Southeast Asia, Australia, Europe, and the Americas, the major themes reflected in everything we heard emerged in a series of discussions with Dr. Catherine Bannerman, the Medical Director of Palliative Care and Hospice at Torrance Memorial Medical Center in Southern California. She and several of her staff members gave us a wondrous and comforting glimpse into the lives of people facing death.

While death is different from life, dying is *not* different from living. "People die the way they live," said Dr. Bannerman. "Their ability to cope with impending death is directly related to the ability they had to make good choices in life. And people who die most calmly are those who continue to make life choices right up to the end."

In fact, as incongruent as it may sound, those who choose the Brilliant Health practices thrive as they are dying. What does Brilliant Health look like as we near death?

Intention

According to the hospice staff, many healthy and life-affirming intentions are hallmarks of a death successfully experienced:

- To enjoy my time right now.

- To live every day as a blessing.

- To focus concerns on my family, rather than on myself.

- To stay active.

- To keep doing what brings pleasure and joy.

- To state out loud how I want to be remembered.

- To create closure with loved ones with whom I've had disagreements.

One of the staff nurses told us, "Many of our patients have the intention to stay alive as long as they can—to see a child again, or go to a grandchild's soccer game, or wait for a brother or sister to arrive from a foreign country. Some of these people live many days or weeks longer than we ever thought possible. Where do they get the physical strength and drive to survive? It has to come from their intentions. There is no other possible source."

A fifty-two-year-old cancer patient had the intention to endure pain as long as possible so he could leave his young child with positive memories of her father. How did this intention come to life? His intention to carefully moderate his medications and to tolerate pain allowed him to take his daughter to Disneyland, where he made a teddy bear with his own voice recorded inside to leave his little girl with a happy message from her dad.

Consider the patients whose intentions about living fully are so compelling they take morphine patches, oxygen tanks, and wheelchairs on cruises. One patient was bed-bound and could only spend a few minutes at a time in a wheelchair but still took his wife on a carefully orchestrated Caribbean cruise so they could enjoy their last anniversary.

Accountability

Even facing death, the healthiest patients pull out of their victim brains into the higher-brain functions. When patients focus only on their symptoms and complain about their pain, according to hospice professionals, they exacerbate their own suffering. They get the entire staff riled up and upset. They may even refuse their medications, and much of their pain is needless. The least successful of them are sadly reminiscent of the Hungry Ghosts.

"Those who thrive have put a lot of thought into the process of dying," said one of the nurses. "Many are actually creative in the ways they approach death. Given the constraint of time, they actively decide how to maximize their time. Even though they're limited by the disease process and they're in bed, just talking about how they plan to die is like taking action. Their words, not actions, become their legacies."

Identification and Centrality

Living our passions while we are dying might seem impractical or completely unrealistic. But Brilliant Health practices are relevant during all phases of our lives. The stories we heard about people doing what they love until the very end are too many to share, but some stand out, such as the writer who converted from a desktop computer to a laptop as he became bedridden, and continued being creative by dictating stories to a scribe when his hands stopped working altogether. Or the woman who loved giving massages and had the nursing staff back up other patients' wheelchairs to hers so she could give them back rubs.

Recasting

Recasting in the world of palliative care is referred to routinely as an *end-of-life review*. Repressed emotions can be terribly hurtful at this point in life, and hospice workers encourage patients who find it difficult to express emotions to share their feelings vividly. "Fear and anger are natural and important," said one social worker. "Love and affection are also abundant during the dying process. Not expressing emotions when you're dying is like robbing yourself of an important part of your own life."

There is also tremendous learning that comes naturally from end-of-life reviews. Dying allows you to look at yourself and your life—to celebrate what you've done well, and to forgive yourself for what hasn't gone as well as you would have liked or would have done differently. As their control over their bodies goes down, patients start to look inward, and they arrive at new meanings and insights. One of the social workers referred to these new meanings as the "lifting of the veil of illusion."

Some of these new understandings are:

• How much we've been loved.

• How much we've loved others.

• How to receive and not just to be the provider.

- What's important, and what's not.

- The need to give up material attachments.

- How to be OK in a not-OK situation.

And from this learning come many opportunities to:

- Fix relationships that need work and reconcile with loved ones.

- Make new emotional connections.

- Right wrongs.

- Enjoy the gifts of others.

- Focus on what is now most important.

- Appreciate and enjoy each day.

- Revel in our abilities to cope and adjust.

Options

At a time when options appear to be shrinking, finding new ways of doing things and new ways of relating to others is essential to allowing people to feel most positive. The truth is: as long as you're conscious, you have options. A hospice nurse summed it up this way: "You have to say to yourself, 'I'm going to die,' and then in the meantime you've got to live. Otherwise, you'll be miserable when you finally go."

Appreciation

Dr. Bannerman said, "The unhappy patients become hyper and say, 'I'm going to die, I'm going to die.' They're so obsessed with the bleak future that they can't possibly stay in the moment and end up torturing themselves with an eventuality they can't control anyway."

The thriving patients appreciate one day at a time. They are not future-focused, using appreciation as a way to stay present. Dr. Bannerman calls this period in the patient's life, *Gift Time Now*. "Life is going to end shortly, and there's nothing that should be taken for granted," she says. "We must focus on now, savor every moment, and this makes every day important and special."

Giving

There are many well-documented cases of people deciding to live well beyond their anticipated day of death. While research doesn't support the notion that we choose our time of death, studies do indicate (see the Giving chapter) that older people who give through acts of service tend to live longer than those who don't give. Hospice nurses, doctors, and social workers tell many magical stories of "the man who said, 'My daughter would feel better if I came to her wedding,' and who then lives until the day after the wedding; or the woman who waits a week to die because, 'my sister is coming from the Philippines in five days and she won't be happy unless she sees me alive'; or 'I have to be by my wife's side at her birthday party.'"

These prolongations of life are driven by the urge to give a gift to others rather than a simple desire for longevity. And this is a time when allowing others to give to us can be the greatest gift of all.

We heard a story about a Japanese-born mother who finally allowed her American-born daughter to feed her in the final days of her life. Though the mother and daughter had had a difficult relationship full of crosscultural conflict, the daughter's recounting of this experience was much like the telling of a miraculous event; each detail of the feeding, told almost as a sacred ritual, had brought the two women together in ways that were entirely new and healing. As the mother died, together the women had experienced a rebirth.

Truth

A sixty-five-year-old kidney cancer patient was completely honest with his family about death. He talked about his spiritual beliefs, his hopes for each family member, his understanding of death, and how much he would have wanted a longer life to participate in the family's future. His truths became the substance of ongoing discussions with loved ones that brought them even closer as a family. And the truth-telling created new bonds among them that were part of his legacy.

A nurse told us, "We professionals are not helping the patient and the families if we're not encouraging them to be open. Everyone in the family system knows the patient is dying, so if you can't talk about it, you're lost. Without stating the truth, the patient becomes isolated in a state of unreality."

So dying well, it turns out, is not really different from living well. In fact, dying well is an important component of a life well lived. And these choices, which so directly enhance our quality of life, will also enhance our process of dying.

When we choose Brilliant Health at any age we are choosing to celebrate life at its fullest with attitudes and behaviors that make us happier, more productive, and healthier. We celebrate our individual selves and fortify our bodies. And, we can take comfort in knowing that we have the opportunity to live in Brilliant Health up until the last breath we take.

Afterword

Through all the years of researching and writing this book, the topic of Brilliant Health has never been anything other than fascinating. And we expect it will be for a long time to come. Its implications are rich and important. Although, at times, we've hit roadblocks and frustrations in our work, it's been a thrilling journey. The world of positive emotions and the impact they have becomes ever more far-reaching. With new brain research coming out all the time, we feel like we're on the tip of an enormous iceberg.

Among all the ideas we've encountered along the way, the relatively new research on neuroplasticity and its downstream affects on the body are the most intriguing and, well, mind-blowing. This gives us hope and the courage to believe that our brains are resilient organs that we can choose to change (and improve!) through our lives. And it's proof of something we've observed in our work for years: that we can change how we behave, enhance our health, and live increasingly richer lives into advanced old age.

To our delight, there are repeated tidal surges of other fascinating research from the social sciences, medicine, and the physical sciences on the overall health benefits of positive affect. Most of these studies weren't available when we began our trek into the world of happiness, and it's all happening so quickly, we expect new research to emerge between the time we finish writing this book and its publication. This data is revolutionizing our modern definition of health, while it brings about unanticipated changes in medical practice. That we now encourage partnerships between doctors and their patients, that patient safety is so highly correlated to human behavior, and that older people are seen as having the potential to live well are all tied to the study of positive emotion and behavior. And that we can now prove how influential happiness is on our health is a lovely substantiation of our grandparents' wisdom.

Throughout our travels, finding Brilliant Health practices firmly established in cultures all over the world has been amazing. The fact that Brilliant Health domains show up in such disparate places has offered abundant proof we are all part of a large, connected, raucous, and sometimes fractious species. That the themes forming the heart of Brilliant Health show up consistently in classical religious and philosophical texts (the Torah, the Bible, the Koran, the Dammaphada, Taoist writings, and others), not to mention worldwide mythologies, is yet another indication of the bonds that hold us together rather than divide us as a human family.

Until just a few days before the final deadline for this

manuscript, we continued to interview Brilliantly Healthy people, and, in fact, gathered data on our oldest interviewee last. And we have no desire to stop anytime soon. In addition to this being one of the most enjoyable parts of our work, stories from real people have illuminated our path from the first inklings that happiness and health were connected. Without the rich picture painted by our storytellers, we couldn't have brought the many little pieces of scientific data to bear on a large, synergistic system of choices and practices.

And, of course, that the Brilliant Health practices are part of a yet larger personal health profile is something we should all remember. Along with our attitudes and behaviors, we can exert control on our nutrition, environmental exposures, and exercise. While there's a great deal we can't control, what's within our grasp is enough to make a significant difference in how we live.

We wish for you great success. Perhaps you'll discover it in a specific Brilliant Health practice. Or maybe the powerful combination of attitudes and behaviors from some or all of the practices will propel you up the staircase. And, if you go on to take the Brilliant Health questionnaire in appendix 1, it's most important to remember that you have the personal power and opportunity to choose to improve your health profile. In any case, we wish you great hope for the future, a powerful happiness, and the physical well-being that comes from Brilliant Health.

Be careful about reading health books. You may die of a misprint.

—MARK TWAIN (1835–1910)

Your Brilliant Health Quotient: A Questionnaire

The following questions will give you an idea of your Brilliant Health Quotient. It's both descriptive and prescriptive, giving you a view of where you are now and providing you with a sense of what you can do specifically to improve your Brilliant Health. This scale is not designed to be an absolute instrument. Your score is unrelated to other people's. It's simply meant to be your personal point of reference. For each of the following statements, please rate your most honest answer on a scale of 0 to 10.

INTENTION

1. I choose my thoughts, feelings, and behaviors before each event of the day.

0	1	2	3	4	5	6	7	8	9	10
strongly										strongly
disagree										agree

ACCOUNTABILITY

2. I don't think of myself as a victim or blame others.

0	1	2	3	4	5	6	7	8	9	10
strongly										strongly
disagree										agree

IDENTIFICATION

3. I envision my passions frequently.

0	1	2	3	4	5	6	7	8	9	10
strongly										strongly
disagree										agree

CENTRALITY

4. I frequently do the things I love to do.

0	1	2	3	4	5	6	7	8	9	10
strongly										strongly
disagree										agree

RECASTING

5. I convert trauma and illness into learning and new opportunities.

0	1	2	3	4	5	6	7	8	9	10
strongly										strongly
disagree										agree

Your Brilliant Health Quotient: A Questionaire

OPTIONS

6. I look for many possibilities as I go through life.

0	1	2	3	4	5	6	7	8	9	10

strongly
disagree

strongly
agree

APPRECIATION

7. I frequently appreciate my life, my body, and I express appreciation to others.

0	1	2	3	4	5	6	7	8	9	10

strongly
disagree

strongly
agree

GIVING

8. I give to others and allow them to give to me.

0	1	2	3	4	5	6	7	8	9	10

strongly
disagree

strongly
agree

TRUTH

9. I tell the truth to myself and others.

0	1	2	3	4	5	6	7	8	9	10

strongly
disagree

strongly
agree

Brilliant Health at Work

Much of our professional life involves applying the Brilliant Health system to groups of people in programs for leadership, wellness, and high-performance team culture. If we believe that elements of good health, high performance, and elevated quality of life for any one individual are also found in human relationships and groups, we can ask, "What does Brilliant Health look like beyond ourselves as individuals—at home, at work, and in our communities?"

This question takes on great significance, not only because so much of our time is spent in personal and work relationships, but because we are evolutionarily designed as small-group mammals and rewarded with healthy biochemicals when our relationships of all types are in order.

In fact, after many years of conducting workshops in global corporations and medical centers, we know that all of our relationships are mediated by the same principles that affect us as individuals. All groups, whether they are teams, corporations, community organizations, families, or marriages are deeply affected by all of the Brilliant Health practices. In fact, the healthiest groups embody each part of this model. And we're equally optimistic about interpersonal relationships. In groups we are highly capable of learning, changing behavior, and making judgments that lead to healthy communal choices.

As we've seen, all of the practices in the Brilliant Health model are synergistic, working together to create an overall feeling of well-being. And we can easily describe a work team or family or organization that integrates these practices into its daily life: it is bristling with energy, full of enthusiasm, able to overcome difficulties, full of self-knowledge and appreciation, flexible, giving, and honest.

Does this sound like a dream team? It is. And it's completely doable. As you learn the Brilliant Health system, remember you can bring these same practices to your relationship with people at work, at school, in your neighborhood, family, and communities.

SELECTED RESEARCH STUDIES

EMBRACING BRILLIANT HEALTH

Benyamini, Y., E. L. Idler, H. Leventhal, and E. A. Leventhal, "Positive Affect and Function as Influences on Self-Assessments of Health: Expanding Our View Beyond Illness and Disability," *Journal of Gerontology: Psychological Sciences* 55B (2000): 107–16.

Brown, W. A., A. D. Sirota, R. Niaura, and T. O. Engebretson, "Endocrine Correlates of Sadness and Elation," *Psychosomatic Medicine* 55 (1993): 458–67.

Chalmers, David J., *The Conscious Mind: In Search of a Fundamental Theory*. Oxford: Oxford University Press, 1996.

Chrousos, G., and P. Gold, "A Healthy Body in a Healthy Mind—and Vice Versa—the Damaging Power of Uncontrollable Stress" (Editorial), *Journal of Clinical Endocrinology and Metabolism* 83 (1998): 1842–45.

DeNeve, K. M., and H. Cooper, "The Happy Personality: A Metaanalysis of 137 Personality Traits and Subjective Well-Being," *Psychological Bulletin* 124 (1998): 197–229.

Diener, E., S. Lyubomirsky, and L. King, "The Benefits of Frequent Positive

Affect: Does Happiness Lead to Success?" *Psychological Bulletin* 131, no. 6 (2005): 803–55.

Flory, J. D., S. B. Manuck, K. A. Matthews, and M. F. Muldoon, "Serotonergic Function in the Central Nervous System Is Associated with Daily Ratings of Positive Mood," *Psychiatry Research* 129, no. 1 (2004): 11–19.

Foster, Rick, and Greg Hicks, *How We Choose to Be Happy*. New York: Putnam, 1999.

Futterman, A. D., M. E. Kemeny, D. Shapiro, W. Polonsky, and J. L. Fahey, "Immunological Variability Associated with Experimentally Induced Positive and Negative Affective States," *Psychological Medicine* 22, no. 1 (1992): 231–38.

Max, D. T., "Happiness 101," *New York Times Magazine*, January 7, 2007.

National Office of Vital Statistics of the United States (NCHS), *Leading Causes of Death, 1900–1998*.

Pressman, S. D., and S. Cohen, "Does Positive Affect Influence Health?" *Psychological Bulletin* 131, no. 6 (2005): 925–71.

CHAPTER 1: INTENTION

Ader, R., and N. Cohen, "Behaviorally Conditioned Immunosuppression," *Psychosomatic Medicine* 37 (1975): 333–40.

Ader, R., D. L. Felten, and N. Cohen, eds., *Psychoneuroimmunology* (vols. 1 and 2, 3rd ed.). San Diego: Academic Press, 2001.

Davidson, R. J., "Well-Being and Affective Style: Neural Substrates and Biobehavioural Correlates," *Philosophical Transactions of the Royal Society of London—Series B: Biological Sciences* 359, no. 1449 (2004): 1395–411.

Doidge, Norman, *The Brain That Changes Itself: Stories of Personal Triumph from the Frontiers of Brain Science*. New York: James H. Silberman Books, 2007.

Haynes, J. D., K. Sakai, G. Rees, S. Gilbert, C. Frith, and D. Passingham, "Reading Hidden Intentions in the Human Brain," *Current Biology* 1, no. 4 (2007): 323–28.

Jonas, Wayne B., and Cindy C. Crawford, eds. *Healing, Intention and Energy Medicine: Science, Research Methods and Clinical Implications*. New York: Elsevier, 2003.

Selected Research Studies

Kiecolt-Glaser, J. K., L. McGuire, T. F. Robles, and R. Glaser, "Psychoneuroimmunology: Psychological Influences on Immune Function and Health," *Journal of Consulting and Clinical Psychology* 70 (2002): 537–47.

Larson, C. L., H. S. Schaefer, G. J. Siegle, C. A. Jackson, M. J. Anderle, and R. J. Davidson, "Fear Is Fast in Phobic Individuals: Amygdala Activation in Response to Fear-Relevant Stimuli," *Biological Psychiatry* 60, no. 4 (2006): 410–17.

Maes, M., D. R. Van Bockstaele, A. Gastel, C. Song, C. Schotte, H. Neels, I. De-Meester, S. Scharpe, and A. Janca, "The Effects of Psychological Stress on Leukocyte Subset Distribution in Humans: Evidence of Immune Activation," *Neuropsychobiology* 39 (1999): 1–9.

Miller, G. E., and S. Cohen, "Psychological Interventions and the Immune System: A Meta-Analytic Review and Critique," *Health Psychology* 20 (2001): 47–63.

Ott, M. J., R. L. Norris, and S. M. Bauer-Wu, "Mindfulness Meditation for Oncology Patients: A Discussion and Critical Review," *Integrative Cancer Therapies* 5, no. 2 (2001): 98–108.

Pine, D. S., "Developmental Psychobiology and Response to Threats: Relevance to Trauma in Children and Adolescents," *Biological Psychiatry* 53, no. 9 (2003): 796–808.

Skinner, R., R. Georgiou, P. Thornton, and N. Rothwell, "Psychoneuroimmunology of Stroke," *Neurologic Clinics* 24, no. 3 (2006): 561–83.

Windmann, S., and T. Kruger, "Subconscious Detection of Threat as Reflected by an Enhanced Response Bias," *Consciousness & Cognition* 7, no. 4 (1998): 603–33.

CHAPTER 2: ACCOUNTABILITY

Carney, R. M., K. E. Freedland, P. K. Stein, G. E. Miller, B. Steinmeyer, M. W. Rich, and S. P. Duntley, "Heart Rate Variability and Markers of Inflammation and Coagulation in Depressed Patients with Coronary Heart Disease," *Journal of Psychosomatic Research* 62, no. 4 (2007): 463–67.

Cousson-Gelie, F., S. Irachabal, M. Bruchon-Schweitzer, J. M. Dilhuydy, and F. Lakdja, "Dimensions of Cancer Locus of Control Scale as Predictors of

Psychological Adjustment and Survival in Breast Cancer Patients," *Psychological Reports* 97, no. 3 (2005): 699–711.

De Faye, B. J., K. G. Wilson, S. Chater, R. A. Viola, and P. Hall, "Stress and Coping with Advanced Cancer," *Palliative & Supportive Care* 4, no. 3 (2006): 239–49.

Graham, J. E., T. F. Robles, J. K. Kiecolt-Glaser, W. B. Malarkey, M. G. Bissell, and R. Glaser, "Hostility and Pain Are Related to Inflammation in Older Adults," *Brain, Behavior, & Immunity* 20, no. 4 (2006): 389–400.

Herbert, T. B., and S. Cohen, "Stress and Immunity in Humans: A Meta-Analytic Review," *Psychosomatic Medicine* 55 (1993): 364–79.

Knüpfer, H., and R. Preiss, "Significance of Interleukin-6 (IL-6) in Breast Cancer" (Review), *Breast Cancer Research & Treatment* 102, no. 2 (2007): 129–35.

Kubacki, A., and K. Jankowski, "Victim Subculture or the 'Poor Me' Syndrome," *Canadian Journal of Psychiatry—Revue Canadienne de Psychiatrie* 41, no. 6 (1996): 414.

Maier, S. F., and L. R. Watkins, "Stressor Controllability, Anxiety and Serotonin," *Cognitive Therapy and Research* 22 (1998): 595–613.

Marmot, M., "Perception of Fairness and Heart Disease" (University College Medical School, Whitehall Study II University College London), *Journal of Epidemiology and Public Health* 61 (2007): 513–18.

Matthews, K. A., B. B. Gump, K. F. Harris, T. L. Haney, and J. C. Barefoot, "Hostile Behavior Predicts Cardiovascular Mortality Among Men Enrolled in the Multiple Risk Factor Intervention Trial," *Circulation* 109 (2004): 66–70.

Miller, T. Q, T. W. Smith, C. W. Turner, M. L. Guijarro, and A. J. Hallet, "A Meta-analytic Review of Research on Hostility and Physical Health," *Psychological Bulletin* 119 (1996): 32–48.

Norra, C., E. C. Skobel, M. Arndt, and P. Schauerte, "High Impact of Depression in Heart Failure: Early Diagnosis and Treatment Options," *International Journal of Cardiology* XX (2007). Available online at www.sciencedirect.com. Accessed January 24, 2008.

Salomons, T. V., T. Johnstone, M. M. Backonja, and R. J. Davidson, "Perceived Controllability Modulates the Neural Response to Pain," *Journal of Neuroscience* 24, no. 32 (2004): 7199–203.

Selected Research Studies

Steppich, B. A., P. Moog, C. Matissek, N. Wisniowski, J. Kuhle, N. Joghetaei, F. J. Neumann, A. Schomig, and I. Ott, "Cytokine Profiles and T Cell Function in Acute Coronary Syndromes," *Atherosclerosis* 190, no. 2 (2007): 443–51.

Thornton, L. M., B. L. Andersen, T. R. Crespin, and W. E. Carson, "Individual Trajectories in Stress Covary with Immunity During Recovery from Cancer Diagnosis and Treatments," *Brain, Behavior, & Immunity* 21, no. 2 (2007): 185–94.

Van Reekum, C. M., H. L. Urry, T. Johnstone, M. E. Thurow, C. J. Frye, C. A. Jackson, H. S. Schaefer, A. L. Alexander, and R. J. Davidson, "Individual Differences in Amygdala and Ventromedial Prefrontal Cortex Activity Are Associated with Evaluation Speed and Psychological Well-Being," *Journal of Cognitive Neuroscience* 19, no. 2 (2007): 237–48.

CHAPTER 3: IDENTIFICATION

Ackerman, C. J., and B. Turkoski, "Using Guided Imagery to Reduce Pain and Anxiety," *Home Healthcare Nurse* 18, no. 8 (2000): 524–30, 531.

Ball, T. M., D. E. Shapiro, C. J. Monheim, et al., "A Pilot Study of the Use of Guided Imagery for the Treatment of Recurrent Abdominal Pain in Children," *Clinical Pediatrics (Philadelphia)* 42, no. 6 (2003): 527–32.

Collins, J. A., and V. H. Rice, "Effects of Relaxation Intervention in Phase II Cardiac Rehabilitation: Replication and Extension," *Heart & Lung* 26, no. 1 (1997): 31–44.

Epstein, G. N., J. P. Halper, E. E. M. Barrett, C. Birdsall, M. McGee, K. P. Baron, and S. Lowenstein, "A Pilot Study of Mind-Body Change in Adults with Asthma who Practice Mental Imagery," *Alternative Therapies and Medicine* 10, no. 4 (2004): 66–71.

Ernst, E., K. Schmidt, and M. Baum, "Complementary/Alternative Therapies for the Treatment of Breast Cancer: A Systematic Review of Randomized Clinical Trials and a Critique of Current Terminology," *The Breast Journal* 12, no. 6 (2006): 526–30.

Fors, E. A., H. Sexton, and K. G. Gotestam, "The Effect of Guided Imagery and Amitriptyline on Daily Fibromyalgia Pain: A Prospective, Randomized, Controlled Trial," *Journal of Psychiatric Research* 36, no. 3 (2002): 179–87.

Gabbay, F. H., D. S. Krantz, W. J. Kop, S. M. Hedges, J. Klein, J. S. Gottdiener, and

Selected Research Studies

A. Rozanski, "Triggers of Myocardial Ischemia During Daily Life in Patients with Coronary Artery Disease: Physical and Mental Activities, Anger and Smoking," *Journal of the American College of Cardiology* 27 (1996): 585–92.

Gruzelier, J. H., "A Review of the Impact of Hypnosis, Relaxation, Guided Imagery and Individual Differences on Aspects of Immunity and Health," *Stress* 5, no. 2 (2002): 147–63.

Khalsa, H. K., "Yoga: An Adjunct to Infertility Treatment," *Fertility & Sterility* 80, no. 4 (2003): 46–51.

Parker, T. S., and K. S. Wampler, "Changing Emotion: The Use of Therapeutic Storytelling," *Journal of Marital & Family Therapy* 32, no. 2 (2006): 155–66.

Reed, T., "Imagery in the Clinical Setting: A Tool for Healing," *Nursing Clinics of North America* 42, no. 2 (2007): 261–77.

Rossman, M. L., "Interactive Guided Imagery as a Way to Access Patient Strengths During Cancer Treatment," *Integrative Cancer Therapies* 1, no. 2 (2002): 162–65.

Rusy, L. M., and S. J. Weisman, "Complementary Therapies for Acute Pediatric Pain Management," *Pediatric Clinics of North America* 47, no. 3 (2000): 589–99.

Sobrinho, L. G., "Prolactin, Psychological Stress and Environment in Humans: Adaptation and Maladaptation," *Pituitary* 6, no. 1 (2003): 35–39.

Toda, M., S. Kusakabe, S. Nagasawa, K. Kitamura, and K. Morimoto, "Effect of Laughter on Salivary Endocrinological Stress Marker Chromogranin A," *Biomedical Research* 28, no. 2 (2007): 115–18.

Wagner, T., et al., "Placebo Effect Studies," NPR interview, August 2007.

Walco, G. A., J. W. Varni, and N. T. Ilowite, "Cognitive-Behavioral Pain Management in Children with Juvenile Rheumatoid Arthritis," *Pediatrics* 89, no. 6 (1992): 1075–79.

Zachariae, R., H. Oster, P. Bjerring, et al., "Effects of Psychologic Intervention on Psoriasis: A Preliminary Report," *Journal of the American Academy of Dermatology* 34, no. 6 (1996): 1008–15.

CHAPTER 4: CENTRALITY

Amat, J., E. Paul, C. Zarza, L. R. Watkins, and S. F. Maier, "Previous Experience with Behavioral Control Over Stress Blocks the Behavioral and Dorsal Raphe

Selected Research Studies

Nucleus Activating Effects of Later Uncontrollable Stress: Role of the Ventral Medial Prefrontal Cortex," *Journal of Neuroscience* 26, no. 51 (2006): 13264–72.

Aspinwall, L. G., "Rethinking the Role of Positive Affect in Self-Regulation," *Motivation and Emotion* 22 (1998): 1–32.

Berk, L. S., D. L. Felten, S. A. Tan, B. B. Bittman, and J. Westengard, "Modulation of Neuroimmune Parameters During the Eustress of Humor-Associated Mirthful Laughter," *Alternative Therapies in Health and Medicine* 7, no. 2 (2001): 62–76.

Cahill, L., and J. L. McGaugh, "A Novel Demonstration of Enhanced Memory Associated with Emotional Arousal," *Consciousness and Cognition* 4 (1995): 410–21.

Cahill, L., and J. L. McGaugh, "Mechanisms of Emotional Arousal and Lasting Declarative Memory," *Trends in Neurosciences* 21 (1998): 294–99.

Cohen, S., C. M. Alper, W. J. Doyle, J. J. Treanor, and R. B. Turner, "Positive Emotional Style Predicts Resistance to Illness After Experimental Exposure to Rhinovirus or Influenza A Virus," *Psychosomatic Medicine* 68, no. 6 (2006): 809–15.

Irwin, M. R., and A. H. Miller, "Depressive Disorders and Immunity: 20 Years of Progress and Discovery," *Brain, Behavior, & Immunity* 21, no. 4 (2007): 374–83.

Koivumaa-Honkanen, H., R. Honkanen, H. Viinamaeki, K. Heikkila, J. Kaprio, and M. Koskenvuo, "Self-Reported Life Satisfaction and 20-Year Mortality in Healthy Finnish Adults," *American Journal of Epidemiology* 152 (2000): 983–91.

Lyubomirsky, S., and L. King, "The Benefits of Frequent Positive Affect: Does Happiness Lead to Success?" *Psychological Bulletin* 131, no. 6 (2005): 803–55.

Olson, M. B., D. S. Krantz, S. F. Kelsey, C. J. Pepine, G. Sopko, E. Handberg, W. J. Rogers, G. L. Gierach, C. K. Mcclure, and C. N. Bairey Merz, "Hostility Scores Are Associated with Increased Risk of Cardiovascular Events in Women Undergoing Coronary Angiography: A Report from the NHLBI-Sponsored WISE Study," *Psychosomatic Medicine* 67 (2005): 546–52.

Suarez, E. C., "Sex Differences in the Relation of Depressive Symptoms, Hostility, and Anger Expression to Indices of Glucose Metabolism in Nondiabetic Adults," *Health Psychology* 25, no. 4 (2006): 484–92.

Selected Research Studies

CHAPTER 5: RECASTING

Anderson, D. E., E. J. Metter, H. Hougaku, and S. S. Najjar, "Suppressed Anger Is Associated with Increased Carotid Arterial Stiffness in Older Adults," *America Journal of Hematology* 19 (2006): 1129–34.

Bacon, S. L., L. L. Watkins, M. Babyak, A. Sherwood, J. Hayano, A. L. Hinderliter, et al., "Effects of Daily Stress on Autonomic Cardiac Control in Patients with Coronary Artery Disease," *American Journal of Cardiology* 93 (2004): 1292–94.

Cohen, S., C. M. Alper, W. J. Doyle, J. J. Treanor, and R. B. Turner, "Positive Emotional Style Predicts Resistance to Illness After Experimental Exposure to Rhinovirus or Influenza A Virus," *Psychosomatic Medicine* 68, no. 6 (2006): 809–15.

Green, R. C., L. A. Cupples, A. Kurz, S. Auerbach, R. Go, D. Sadovnick, R. Duara, W. A. Kukull, H. Chui, T. Edeki, P. A. Griffith, R. P. Friedland, D. Bachman, and L. Farrer, "Depression as a Risk Factor for Alzheimer Disease: The MIRAGE Study," *Archives of Neurology* 60, no. 5 (2003): 753–59.

Kelley, K. W., R. M. Bluthe, R. Dantzer, J. H. Zhou, W. H. Shen, R. W. Johnson, and S. R. Broussard, "Cytokine-Induced Sickness Behavior," *Brain Behavior & Immunity* 17 (2003): S112–118.

Marks, I., and A. Tobena, "Learning and Unlearning Fear: A Clinical and Evolutionary Perspective," *Neuroscience & Biobehavioral Reviews* 14, no. 4 (1990): 365–84.

Moskowitz, A. K., "'Scared stiff': Catatonia as an Evolutionary-Based Fear Response," *Psychological Review* 111, no. 4 (2004): 984–1002.

Peters, M. L., M. Sommer, J. M. de Rijke, F. Kessels, E. Heineman, J. Patijn, M. A. Marcus, J. W. Vlaeyen, and M. van Kleef, "Somatic and Psychologic Predictors of Long-Term Unfavorable Outcome After Surgical Intervention," *Annals of Surgery* 245, no. 3 (2007): 487–94.

Ramfelt, E., E. Severinsson, and K. Lutzen, "Attempting to Find Meaning in Illness to Achieve Emotional Coherence: The Experiences of Patients with Colorectal Cancer," *Cancer Nursing* 25, no. 2 (2002): 141–49.

Spiegel, D., J. R. Bloom, H. C. Kraemer, E. Gottheil, "Effect of Psychosocial Treatment on Survival of Patients with Metastatic Breast Cancer," *Lancet* 14, no. 2 (1989): 888–91.

Selected Research Studies

CHAPTER 6: OPTIONS

Bracha, H. S., "Freeze, Flight, Fight, Fright, Faint: Adaptationist Perspectives on the Acute Stress Response Spectrum," *CNS Spectrums* 9, no. 9 (2004): 679–85.

Davidson, P. M., K. Dracup, J. Phillips, J. Daly, and G. Padilla, "Preparing for the Worst While Hoping for the Best: The Relevance of Hope in the Heart Failure Illness Trajectory," *Journal of Cardiovascular Nursing* 22, no. 3 (2007): 159–65.

Duggleby, W. D., L. Degner, A. Williams, K. Wright, D. Cooper, D. Popkin, and L. Holtslander, "Living with Hope: Initial Evaluation of a Psychosocial Hope Intervention for Older Palliative Home Care Patients," *Journal of Pain and Symptom Management* 33, no. 3 (2007): 247–57.

Giltay, E. J., M. H. Kamphuis, S. Kalmijn, F. G. Zitman, and D. Kromhout, "Dispositional Optimism and the Risk of Cardiovascular Death: The Zutphen Elderly Study," *Archives of Internal Medicine* 166, no. 4 (2006): 431–36.

Kivimaki, M., J. Vahtera, M. Elovainio, H. Helenius, A. Singh-Manoux, and J. Pentti, "Optimism and Pessimism as Predictors of Change in Health After Death or Onset of Severe Illness in Family," *Health Psychology* 24, no. 4 (2005): 413–21.

Peters, M. L., M. Sommer, J. M. de Rijke, F. Kessels, E. Heineman, J. Patijn, M.A.E. Marcus, J.W.S. Vlaeyen, and M. van Kleef, "Somatic and Psychologic Predictors of Long-Term Unfavorable Outcome After Surgical Intervention," *Annals of Surgery* 245, no. 3 (2007): 487–94.

Rasmussen, H. N., C. Wrosch, M. F. Scheier, and C. S. Carver, "Self-Regulation Processes and Health: The Importance of Optimism and Goal Adjustment," *Journal of Personality* 74 (2006): 6.

Schofield, P., D. Ball, J. G. Smith, R. Borland, P. O'Brien, S. Davis, I. Olver, G. Ryan, and D. Joseph, "Optimism and Survival in Lung Carcinoma Patients," *Cancer* 100, no. 6 (2004): 1276–82.

Winterling, J., E. Wasteson, B. Sidenvall, E. Sidenvall, B. Glimelius, P. O. Sjoden, and K. Nordin, "Relevance of Philosophy of Life and Optimism for Psychological Distress Among Individuals in a Stage Where Death Is Approaching," *Supportive Care in Cancer* 14, no. 4 (2006): 310–19.

CHAPTER 7: APPRECIATION

Arias, A. J., K. Steinberg, A. Banga, and R. L. Trestman, "Systematic Review of the Efficacy of Meditation Techniques as Treatments for Medical Illness," *Journal of Alternative & Complementary Medicine* 12, no. 8 (2006): 817–32.

Cloninger, C. R., "Spirituality and the Science of Feeling Good," *Southern Medical Journal* 100, no. 7 (2007): 740–43.

Ditto, B., M. Eclache, and N. Goldman, "Short-Term Autonomic and Cardiovascular Effects of Mindfulness Body Scan Meditation," *Annals of Behavioral Medicine* 32, no. 3 (2006): 227–34.

Hollander, E., J. Bartz, W. Chaplin, A. Phillips, J. Sumner, L. Soorya, E. Anagnostou, and S. Wasserman, "Oxytocin Increases Retention of Social Cognition in Autism," *Biological Psychiatry* 61 (2007): 498–503.

Kashdana, T. B., G. Uswatteb, and T. Julian, "Gratitude and Hedonic and Eudaimonic Well-Being in Vietnam War Veterans," *Behaviour Research and Therapy* 44 (2006): 177–99.

Kendrick, K. M., "The Neurobiology of Social Bonds," *Journal of Neuroendocrinology* 16, no. 12 (2004): 1007–08.

Kiss, A., and J. D. Mikkelsen, "Oxytocin—Anatomy and Functional Assignments: A Minireview," *Endocrine Regulations* 39, no. 3 (2005): 97–105.

Meinlschmidt, G., and C. Heim, "Sensitivity to Intranasal Oxytocin with Early Parental Separation," *Biological Psychiatry* 61 (2007): 1109–11.

Rousseau, P., "Living in the Present," *American Journal of Hospice & Palliative Care* 21, no. 6 (2004): 467–68.

Slagter, H. A., A. Lutz, L. L. Greischar, A. D. Francis, S. Nieuwenhuis, et al., "Mental Training Affects Distribution of Limited Brain Resources," *PLoS Biology* 5, no. 6 (2007): e138.

Toledo-Pereyra, L. H., "Gratitude," *Journal of Investigative Surgery* 19, no. 3 (2006): 137–40.

CHAPTER 8: GIVING

Berkman, L. F., "The Role of Social Relations in Health Promotion," *Psychosomatic Medicine* 57 (1995): 245–54.

Coan, J. A., H. S. Schaefer, and R. J. Davidson, "Lending a Hand: Social Regulation of the Neural Response to Threat," *Psychological Science* 17, no. 12 (2006): 1032–39.

Davidson, R. J., J. Kabat-Zinn, et al., "Alterations in Brain and Immune Function Produced by Mindfulness Meditation," *Psychosomatic Medicine* 65 (2003): 564–70.

Fox, A. S., T. R. Oakes, S. E. Shelton, A. K. Converse, R. J. Davidson, and N. H. Kalin, "Calling for Help Is Independently Modulated by Brain Systems Underlying Goal-Directed Behavior and Threat Perception," *Proceedings of the National Academy of Sciences of the United States of America* 102, no. 11 (2005): 4176–79.

Fredrickson, B. L., and R. W. Levenson, "Positive Emotions Speed Recovery from the Cardiovascular Sequelae of Negative Emotions," *Cognition & Emotion* 12 (1998): 191–220.

Hainsworth, J., and J. Barlow, "Volunteers' Experiences of Becoming Arthritis Self-Management Lay Leaders: 'It's Almost as If I've Stopped Aging and Started to Get Younger!' " *Arthritis & Rheumatism* 45, no. 4 (2001): 378–83.

Ironson, G., R. Stuetzle, and M. A. Fletcher, "An Increase in Religiousness/Spirituality Occurs After HIV Diagnosis and Predicts Slower Disease Progression Over 4 Years in People with HIV," *Journal of General Internal Medicine* 21, no. 5 (2006): 562–68.

Moll, J., F. Krueger, R. Zahn, M. Pardini, R. de Oliveira-Souza, and J. Grafman, "Human Fronto-Mesolimbic Networks Guide Decisions About Charitable Donation," *Proceedings of the National Academy of Sciences of the United States of America* 103, no. 42 (2006): 15623–28.

Williams, K. D., "Ostracism," *Annual Review of Psychology* 58 (2007): 425–52.

CHAPTER 9: TRUTH

Abe, N., M. Suzuki, E. Mori, M. Itoh, and T. Fujii, "Deceiving Others: Distinct Neural Responses of the Prefrontal Cortex and Amygdala in Simple Fabrication and Deception with Social Interactions," *Journal of Cognitive Neuroscience* 19, no. 2 (2007): 287–95.

DasGupta, S., "Being John Doe Malkovich: Truth, Imagination, and Story in Medicine," *Literature and Medicine* 25, no. 2 (2006): 439–62.

Selected Research Studies

Bond, Gary D., "Deception Detection Expertise," *Law and Human Behavior* 10 (2007). Available online at www.springerlink.com/content/3851143983032195. Accessed January 24, 2008.

Erdem, F., "Optimal Trust and Teamwork: From Groupthink to Teamthink," *Work Study* 52, no. 5 (2003): 229–33.

Haidt, J., "The New Synthesis in Moral Psychology," *Science* 316, no. 5827 (2007): 998–1002.

Lee, T. M., H. L. Liu, L. H. Tan, C. C. Chan, S. Mahankali, C. M. Feng, J. Hou, P. T. Fox, and J. Gao, "Lie Detection by Functional Magnetic Resonance Imaging," *Human Brain Mapping* 15, no. 3 (2002): 157–64.

INDEX

Index

blaming/victimhood, 53–58
    defensive blaming behavior and, 53,
        56–58
    fate and, 63–67
    genetics and, 63–67
    immune response and, 55
    physical effects of, 54–58
    professional victims and, 67–68
    research studies on, 53–54
    as social disease, 53
bliss
    insomnia and, 74–75
    Intensive Bliss Therapy and, 76
    pain and, 76–77
    stress/stress-related diseases and, 76
Bliss List
    BIQ and, sharpening, 72–73
    building, 71–72
    Centrality and, 93, 95, 98, 102
    Identification and, 213, 223
    imagery and, 81
Body-Booster, 38
body intelligence quotient (BIQ),
    72–73
brain/brain function
    Accountability and, 62–63
    active thought and, 25
    analysis and, 25
    appreciative, 157
    attention deficit and, 157
    chemical reactions and, 25–26, 55, 71,
        168
    consciousness and, 25, 26
    envisioning and, 79–80
    Giving and, 174
    higher, 25–26, 32, 99, 139, 231
    imagery and, 74
    lower, 25–26, 32, 55
    messages from your body and, 73
    neuroplasticity and, 26
    Options and, 135–136
    pathways to, opening, 27–28
    subconscious intentions and, 48–49
    unconscious intentions and, 31–33

    victim brain and, 54–58, 231
    see also research studies
breast cancer. *See* cancer
Brilliant Health, embracing, 1–19
    choosing, 7
    complexity of health and, 9–11
    creation of (authors'), 14–19, 237–39
    cultural, worldwide, 238
    development and perfection of, 6–7
    immune response and, 10
    innovative programs and, creation of,
        17
    medicine and, evolution of, 11–14
    outcomes of, 6
    practices of, 5–6
    psychological rewards of, 8–9
    research studies on, 17
    teaching of, 14, 18
    see also stories/interviews
Brilliant Health, nine practices of
    Accountability, 51–69
    Appreciation, 154–70
    Centrality, 92–110
    Giving, 171–188
    Identification, 70–91
    Intention, 23–50
    Options, 135–53
    Recasting, 111–34
    Truth, 189–208
    see also individual headings
Brilliant Health Research Instrument
    (HIP-10), 123–24
Brilliant Health workshops, 18
bubonic plague, 12
burnout, 6
Burns, George, 93

cancer
    breast, 115–16, 149–51, 180
    colonoscopies and, 183
    colorectal cancer, 44–46
    diagnosis (anticipating), 161–62
    embracing Brilliant Health and, 6
    leukemia, 107–8

Index

Index

Index

Index

Index

Index

Index

Index

For information about our training programs and keynote
speeches, please contact us at
info@fosterhicks.com,
or visit our website at
www.ChoosingBrilliantHealth.com.